CREATING
AN
ENCHANTED
PLACE

THE
SECRET
IN THE CLASSROOM

Sylvia Boltz Tucker

CREATING AN ENCHANTED PLACE

REFOUNDING EDUCATION

THE *SECRET*

IN THE CLASSROOM

Sylvia Boltz Tucker

True North Publications
San Marcos, California

FOR TEACHERS, STUDENTS, AND PARENTS:

A NEW WAY TO LOOK INSIDE THE CLASSROOM

AND LEARNING PLACES WITH THE *SECRET*

ILLUSTRATIONS BY
    DONALD A. LOVE-BOLTZ
    SYLVIA BOLTZ TUCKER

Published by
True North Publications
San Marcos, California, U.S.A.
www.truenorthpublications.com
Printed in the U.S.A.

Cover design by Sylvia Boltz Tucker
Book design by Sylvia Boltz Tucker

Printed in the United States of America

First Printing: August 2010

ISBN-13: 978-0-9844837-0-9

Contents

ACKNOWLEDGMENTS

When your journey has been such a joy and has lasted so long, where do you begin to give your thanks and how do you find the words to express your gratitude for the food and drink along the way?

There have been so many who have contributed to the thoughts, concepts, and ideas I have chosen to "put to pen." That expression itself belies the travel from pen to computer. I have lived in and through incredible times that have shaped me. I was born toward the end of the first great world war; I served in the Navy during the second great world war. I have felt the pain when you have two sons of draft age during the Vietnam War and you don't know what their future will bring. These things have formed me.

I was born into a strict German culture. I am grateful to my mother and father for the values and expectations that they instilled. My extended family, which was very large, was support at so many junctures in the road. I am grateful for the diversity that existed in my area. Thanks to all the different individuals and groups that taught me tolerance and acceptance.

My teachers and coaches through grade school and high school were special people who taught me confidence, courage, perseverance, and academic integrity. Thank you all... with a special thank you to Coach Eddie. You allowed me to be me, to develop my talents, and to be true to what I believed.

My two sons have been special soul mates throughout our lives together. They have remained my greatest encouragement and my most honest critics. They have picked me up when I needed that, and they have kept me grounded when I needed that. But most of all we have always known and felt unconditional love and respect. Models are the strongest teachers. Thank you, Bob and Britt. And thank you, Britt, for listening to me as I read you page after page; your suggestions were filled with their usual insight.

My digital generation grandchildren are amazing. They have kept me young at heart and young of mind. Thank you Colin, Kera, Hailey and Cassidy. You are truly inspirational. You all are true sons and daughters of life's longing for itself. You teach me that lesson anew every day.

I would not know how to thank the many sources of my knowledge. So many of the ideas and concepts have come from so many mentors and authors. To trace a single source would be very difficult when much has come from so many. I have tried to give credit where I felt comfortable about the origin of the material. Often the material is an amalgam of readings, experiences, and conversations. It is difficult, for instance, to remember exactly where I learned what from Fritjof Capra from his books, his lectures and presentation, or our conversations. The same is true of Bob Samples, Peter Senge, Madeline Hunter, or Warren Bennis, and so many more. There are so many more great books, conversations, and incredible people who have influenced me on my journey. I am grateful to you all. If I have failed to acknowledge something or someone, I did so unknowingly.

I want to give special thanks to Hendrik Gideonse, Mary Blizzard, Pam Eves, and Jim Brown, who read the manuscript and gave me invaluable information and suggestions. Special thanks to Debbie Brown who helped to make it camera ready.

To all my students over the more than sixty years of my teaching career must go special thanks for keeping me on the path of learning. To all of my colleagues over the years, I say thanks.

Some of the illustrations are a gift from my nephew, Donald A. Love-Boltz. It took someone who knew me well and who knew my early environments to take the images from my mind and put them to paper so beautifully. Thank you, Donnie.

Thanks to Walt Disney and all the imagineers for "imagineering." It has become a word in our culture.

The work of Rhonda Byrne and others brought The *Secret* in word and image to so many. The applications for education hold much promise. Thank you all.

My gratitude for my Christian faith is given to the many along the way who taught me by example and by word what faith means. My mother was the greatest of these inspirations and teachers. There were many along the trek and they continue to be in my life. My father showed me how to believe in myself, and how to be confident to reach for the stars.

INTRODUCTION

I LOOK BACK AND I WONDER...

I wonder... why people ask me why I'm still working... why learning is such a chore for some... why such a natural process as learning is so painful for some and joyful for others... how each new day brought surprises and amazement... how each new sunset brought more interesting colors and shapes... how each starry night brought more stars to the sky because I took the time to look... why I had to learn so many times to take time to smell the roses... how much fun it has been to learn about technology from tech natives, my grandchildren... how fast technology will change the world of these technology natives...what happened to all those excited faces that I saw in my classrooms... but I also wonder what happened to all those blank and disinterested faces I saw in classrooms I visited.

Public schools are in troubled waters, troubled monopolistic waters. Many feel public schools cannot be fixed because of the structure. Schools are government owned and government operated monopolies that are populated with learners who are forced to attend. Parents cannot, for the most part, even send their children to any school in their district; they have a designated school and must get an intradistrict transfer if they choose another school than the one designated.

For more than eighty years I have been a rider on the merry-go-round called education. Experts with many ideas have jumped off and on. The dashing horses have been painted new colors and given new names. Sometimes the horses were replaced with elegant carriages. But the music didn't change much; the same melodic sounds remind you that it is still a merry-go-round. People come and ride because it is nostalgic. Workers come and go and try to change the music, but powerful groups like the music as it is.

The monopoly continues. Before compulsory education, literacy rates were higher than before this compulsory monopoly was created. Millions of Americans over the age of sixteen can't read or fill in simple applications with personal data. Many can't write simple letters or messages or do simple arithmetic problems. This monopoly has created a system of protections for unfit, unwilling, and non-productive personnel. Unions not only protect these people, but they make it difficult for the great committed people to do their jobs. Student learning suffers. It is a puzzle, but the puzzle doesn't have many pieces.

There is a local union supported by a state union supported by a national union supported by union philosophy in general. There are members in all these unions, many who would not belong to unions if they had a choice. These are the wonderful professionals who are committed and passionate about their work. They spend their time and energy helping young people accomplish their dreams. But their environment is clouded by the demands of the negotiations, the multi-level government requirements, and the malaise of many who are forced into this monopolistic monolith, public education.

In addition, the more that we try to be all things to all people, the less we are to anyone. State directed curriculum and state and national testing have added great burdens for our teachers and students. Legislation is passed because of pressure from one group or another. Trying to meet the various directives buries educators under mountains of paperwork that take valuable time from teaching and learning activities.

One might ask how this entity stays in business, why parents don't make other choices. Public schools are protected with government compulsion. Children are forced to attend; parents are forced to pay school taxes, school boards must negotiate with the unions, and unions oppose any school choice options that appear. In addition, private schools are out of the reach financially of most families. Charter schools particularly are opposed by the unions and, therefore, by many teachers who enlist the aid of their students' parents to also oppose them.

Until this monopoly is broken, or by some magic, choice becomes a viable option for all, our merry-go-round will see only surface changes, new paint, a new melody here and there. The price for our young learners may become more critical. We now must add the fact that we have a carousel not only not suited to many riders of the last century, but one now playing music that is not even recognized by the natives of the digital learners of the 21st century.

It is for all of these incredible natives like my grandchildren and the thousands of other 21st century learners that this immigrant to the digital generation writes these words. I have spent my professional life trying to make this monopoly less monopolistic, less compulsive, less governmental, and less servile. I put forth my ideas with joy and enthusiasm. I know that the human spirit is alive; the desire to learn is alive. I know that I have learned to negotiate the shoals of the troubled waters. I know that there are many who teach and learn with passion and purpose. They create the tapestries of their classrooms from the vibrations of the positive energy of their learners. But we must have this for all learners.

There are laws of the universe that supersede the laws of government and the control of unions. There are professionals of good will and amazing talent who find their way around the regulations and policies that hurt learners. They are willing to risk their jobs to protect the precious humanity and dignity of the persons in their charge. They view these learners as whole, priceless, and holy. And so do I.

"These children are not our children," as Poet Kahlil Gibran has stated so well, "They are the sons and daughters of life's longing for itself." They all deserve an enchanted place in which to learn.

P. S.
Before I could get this document to press, I was given another opportunity to strengthen the lessons I have learned.

A friend called me and asked me to talk with her son and daughter-in-law. These two young people turning thirty are both "college dropouts." They are searching for meaning in an educational system that consistently denied them an enchanted place for learning. They wanted a degree; they wanted to pursue their education, but could not tolerate a system that was devoid of meaning for them. Where could they find a system that would allow them to think, rather than parrot a professor's thoughts? Where would they find classes and university experiences that held meaning for their development as they knew it should happen for them? Where could they pursue a program of study that would allow them the credentials to teach others, to help others find meaning in their education? Every day they interacted with, worked with, did business with, or communicated with people who were woefully lacking critical thinking skills.

What were they to do? How could they rekindle the motivation, the energy, and the passion for learning that they possessed in their personal beings? How could they meet the demands of institutions that had already decided what they needed? They only had to comply with the rules, regulations, and policies. But they had come too far in their selfness to pursue that path again.

We talked about the enchantment of learning. They agreed. We discussed where they wanted to go, how they wanted to serve, and how they hoped to make a difference in people's lives. We outlined what would make their educational experiences exciting again. We talked about changing our thinking.

This new thinking would be about the possibilities, not the limitations. The new thoughts would be about building the educational house of enchantment from the pieces of passion for learning that lie dormant. It would be about using building blocks of interest and experience, newness and challenge. It would be about a new design, a self-design that fits the nature and needs of the builder. Only new materials and creative design would be allowed.

But what about the regulations, policies, sterility, and inflexibility they had experienced? They would require positive action and thought when encountered. Creating a personal program would be first. Pursuing and implementing can only come from the sureness and passion of the creation.

The conversation pursued many avenues; it continued through wonder, excitement, joy, and to let's go do it. They had changed their thinking in a very short period of time. They were ready to make their enchanted place happen. I realized during those moments, that it is for the multitude of disenchanted and for the people who provide or destroy learning environments that I have written about the classroom as "AN ENCHANTED PLACE."

PROLOGUE

Any path is only a path, and there is no affront,
to oneself or to others,
in dropping it if that is what your heart tells you.
Look at every path closely and deliberately.
Try it as many times as you think necessary.
Then ask yourself, and yourself alone one question.
Does this path have a heart?
If it does, the path is good. If it doesn't, it is of no use.
Carlos Castenada

It has taken many soul-searching hours, days and years to learn what I am saying in this book. I have read and re-read the pages to know if the words have a heart. All the words come from my beliefs about people as whole and holy. I believe that I have truly taught when I have touched the soul of another, when I have made a positive difference because I have been there.

The Universe, God, Source has been a magnanimous teacher. When I was ready to learn, a teacher always appeared in physical body, or in a book, or a relationship. It might be a conversation, an airport traveler, a conference, a speech. Teachers have inhabited my universe whenever I was ready for the lesson. I came to this earth with the capacity to learn, the eagerness to learn. I was given the physical and mental capacity for excellence and humanity; I was given the capacity for energy to pursue dreams and aspirations. I was given the mind and soul to test each path for heart.

You will recognize the teachers and the lessons in much of what you read. You will feel the search for the heart in the paths.

7

CHAPTER 1

IN THE BEGINNING

As I walked the campus at Iowa State Teachers College in Cedar Falls, Iowa in the fall of 1941, I contemplated my upcoming trip. As a representative of Kappa Delta Pi, I would board the train in Iowa and travel across the Great Plains, over the soaring mountains, and down across the fertile California valley into the beautiful city of San Francisco, the city by the magnificent Golden Gate Bridge.

What an adventure for a small town farm girl from the hills and rivers of northeastern Iowa. I had been as far as the noisy streets and the belching smoke of industry in South Bend, Indiana. San Francisco was another matter. The change from the brown grass and resting trees of fall and winter in Iowa to the swaying palms and green grass of California was environmental shock.

The train ride was an adventure in so many ways. Sleeping in a Pullman car and figuring out how to get dressed while lying on my back in the upper bunk was a wonderful challenge. Watching the miles roll by while eating in the diner was fun. Great conversations were possible about my chosen profession—teaching—while relaxing in the club car.

There were many superintendents on my train who were going to their annual association meeting in San Francisco. I found myself engaged several times in philosophical discussions about teaching and learning. As I look back, I realize that I knew enough to feel confident in these discussions. One of these discussions was with the superintendent from Aberdeen, South Dakota. It certainly did not occur to me that it was any more than that—a discussion with an interesting person.

The result was quite different. Within a few days of my return to campus, I was presented with a contract to teach high school biology and senior and junior high physical education in Aberdeen for the yearly salary of $1,200. I realize now that my majors in physical education and business education and my minors in English and biological science were like a treasure trove for anyone hiring. I could teach four disciplines. I accepted the job and as we all seem to enjoy saying, "The rest is history."

AT LAST—THE JOB

After graduating from Iowa State Teachers College, now the University of Northern Iowa, I made my way to South Dakota in the fall of 1942 as a new, very young, no-experience teacher in a district where I was informed that only teachers with five or more years of experience were hired. I found out quite early what that meant—the older, wiser, experienced teachers took turns taking me aside to "help" me get adjusted.

They informed me about the rules and particularly where I should and should not go and where I should and should not be seen. My curiosity and interest caused me to explore why those "forbidden" places were off-limits to teachers. Obviously, common sense put some out-of-bounds. Others I found exceedingly interesting; they were where kids liked to hang out to have fun.

CENTRAL HIGH

Central High School and Junior High looked and felt pretty much like hundreds of schools in our country. They had rooms and chairs and tables that generally faced toward the teacher's desk or table which occupied its usual place in the front of the room. Students filed or piled in for their period of joy, pain, or indifference. They had staircases that were designated "up stairs" and "down stairs." They had students scurrying from class to class. They had a principal's office with kids waiting to see the principal. They had music and laughter and kids stopping to swap last night's news.

They had cheerleaders, and the excitement of game days. Central High had boys' football and basketball teams and other male sports, but no girls' teams. Because I had come from Iowa where girls played basketball and softball on regular school teams, I found it disappointing that there were no girls' teams at Central.

Yes, it could have been a school located in hundreds of communities in our nation. Well, except in pheasant season when pheasants rule. Pheasant season in South Dakota was a cultural happening. Kids would be "absent" to hunt pheasant and somehow would hope to take care of the situation with a gift of pheasant for the teacher. At least, I had wonderful pheasant dinners. It was a wonderful place to start teaching; the kids were great, the town was friendly and respected its teachers; and I was given freedom to pursue my dreams.

Probably the greatest difficulty that I experienced was trying to go up the "down staircase." I had physical education classes in the basement and biology classes on the third floor; in addition, the classes were alternated. My biology class was on the same end of the building as my P.E. office, but three floors up. Because I had to change clothes between classes to be presentable for each class, I had little time to get to the next class; the only way that I could get to class on time was going up the "down stairs."

Yes, for some time, I was stopped by each new stair monitor or yelled at to go back and go up or down the correct stairs. Since I had students in my classes who were as old as I, I came to understand that my youth, just 21, was a real problem for the important job of stair monitors.

Our first teaching job becomes etched in our minds. My etching is a happy one. The challenges and joys brought personal growth and respect and most of all deep gratitude for the opportunity and special gratitude for the many people in my life who had given me the courage, curiosity, strength, energy, humanity, and desire for excellence.

When I walked into my first class of 72 junior high kids in physical education, I could have been overwhelmed, but I thought my job was to create the best environment for the kids I was given. I realize now that I created immediate learning centers. I had kids in several different places doing different things. It worked out well. Oddly, no one taught me about learning centers; I don't think the terms had been invented yet. Creating places where kids can learn is the task whether you have two or seventy-two. So I did.

THE DECADES ROLL

When I started teaching sixty-seven years ago, I remembered the kind of learning environment in which I thrived, the kind of environment and behavior that shot learners down, and the kind of place that brought out the best. I remembered the learning places that produced wonder and excitement that showed in learners' faces, the kind of place you went away from saying, "Wow, that was funnnnnnnn!" You knew because you wanted to go back tomorrow and the next day. That was the kind of environment I wanted to create.

I remembered that when I felt like running, like hurrying to that place, when I had a smile on my face and joy in my heart, and my soul was happy and eager to touch others, I knew I wanted to be there. But it wasn't just me. I could touch the happiness of others; we could join in our joy and eagerness for learning. We talked about what we learned; we helped each other. We shared our visions and dreams because we were safe to do so. No one there was allowed to devastate our dreams or visions.

When you knew that the sun was up beyond the rain, when you knew that the sun was coming through the fog, when your morning was filled with expectation and excitement, you knew! When I got to school and the wonderful man who rang our school bell each morning said, "Good morning, you're here early." I knew he cared. I always got there early because it was a place I wanted to be. What was the secret?

Yes, I was even eager when I ran behind the horse-drawn bus that I rode to school in New Albin, Iowa. I ran behind in the winter to try to keep warm. Mother would send a hot brick or a warm bag of salt to help, but they never kept me warm the whole way. My hands and feet would be cold by the time Mr. George Hayes, the bus driver,

would "giddy-up" his horses to school. But the room was warm and the radiator would dry my wet mittens and radiate welcome heat to my very cold hands and feet.

I wish that I could show you a picture of the school bus, but none exists. It was a big rectangular, wooden wagon box with seats on the side and a door on the back and Mr. Hayes up front.

Mr. Hayes was a good driver who always deposited us safely at the schoolhouse door.

"Here we are," he would say as he commanded the horses with an emphatic, "Whoa!"

"See you this afternoon," he would shout as we scrambled toward the door.

"Good morning, Sylvia." My teacher's voice and smile told me it was a place of good mornings. "Glad you're here!" I felt the joy of acceptance.

SCHOOL, THE MAGICAL PLACE

School was this magical place. It was a rainbow in my life. I had few books at home. At school I had so many wonderful books. I could travel to such marvelous places. I could point my finger at any place on the big globe in my schoolroom and go there in my mind. I could ask my teacher for information about a place so I could decide when I wanted to take my imaginary journey.

I could read about people and places, ships with tall sails, castles and mountains, strange creatures I would someday see, and little girls on their way to school as they walked by windmills and tulips or rice fields or pyramids. Some of them looked a little different but inside I somehow knew that we were not different about our desire to learn and learn and know and know. We were all connected.

And then there was the wonderful one-room school I attended in early elementary school. My sister and I walked the mile plus almost every day. How exciting a place it was. I not only had my "grade level" books and work, I had access to all the rest, too.

All I had to do was listen to what the older kids were working on or I could go sit with them and work on the lessons with them, I guess I devised my own Individual Learning Plan.

I could pursue any of the exciting things going on around me. I created my own Ungraded School. No one told me that I was too young, or that it wasn't my grade or that I should take my own seat. There was just one requirement—I had to have the work assigned to me finished. I was highly motivated to finish my work fast; I did not want to have anything stand in the way of the world being available to me. What was the secret of this magical place called my school?

As a third grader, I felt so lucky when my parents bought me a mellophone, the early French horn, and my sister a saxophone. We would sit for hours on our front lawn under a great big tree and toot away. Toot, toot, toot! Fortunately, no one made a practice schedule for us or restricted our time. Since we lived on a farm no one was within hearing distance—only the creatures and animals that sometimes passed by or dared to peek out from a hiding place. We could experience the joy of listening to the sounds come back to us from the surrounding hills. We marveled at the return sound; the hills sent them back faithfully and with great fidelity.

Once in a while we would be enticed from our practice to take a ride in the great swing that hung in the mammoth tree that was our canopy. The limb from which the swing hung was very high. As you dipped and rose with the arc of the swing, you had a wee sense of what birds must feel as they swoop and rise in midair.

At the end of the summer, the company that sold us the instruments wanted to take my sister and me on a tour to other schools to demonstrate how much progress could be made on an instrument in six weeks, and demonstrate what could be accomplished with "hard work." What was the secret of two kids willing to make such a commitment to learning?

"Sylvia, you're such a good speller. You'll win a contest someday," my eighth-grade teacher said. My teacher believed and expected and her thoughts and words were delivered. I believed and expected. that I could. And I did. I won the county written spelling contest. What is the secret of such expectation?

My high school was small, 25 in my class. But I never felt that small was a disadvantage for me. Perhaps the curriculum was limited and the extracurricular offerings not as plentiful. But since I had no experience in a large school, I had no way to know the difference. I always felt advantaged. I knew everyone and everyone knew me. I had classes with every teacher in the building.

I took every class available. I played on the basketball and softball teams, played in the band, sang in glee club and small groups, edited the school paper, worked for the superintendent, was lab assistant in chemistry, and did any other job that needed to be done. I thought only about the opportunities and when I ran out of opportunities and classes, I studied classes during the summer not offered during the school year. My teachers were excited when I asked for books and work during the summer.

Yes, I still had time for fishing, excursions on the paddle wheel boats that plied the Mississippi River, time with my cousins at my grandpa's immense farm, and time to ride my pony. There was time to pick berries with my dad, play with my younger brother, attend the yearly carnival, and anything else that ventured into my neighborhood during the summer.

In the midst of all this joyful adventure, I must admit that there were times when I would be reminded by some that I was just a kid from the country. It was obvious that we had little money, fewer clothes than most, and a rented home for most of my school years. That only made me work harder.

THE RIGHT PARENTS

Wayne Dyer, author and lecturer, talks about being born to the right set of parents, in the right place, at the right time. I concur. I know that I was born to the right set of parents, Peter and Alvina Meyer Boltz, on a farm on the Sand Cove near the small, small town of New Albin, Iowa. I was given the right older sister, Esther, and right younger brother, DeVillo. And I was blessed to be born into a family of many aunts, uncles and cousins.

My grandfather, George Meyer, on my mother's side of the family, was a stern German man. I only learned to understand German in order to know what he was saying at the dinner table or anywhere else I might encounter him. Grandpa Meyer had come from Germany as a young man "with only his knapsack." He was a very successful farmer; he acquired much land and built a big farm with many big buildings, including the three-family home in which I was born.

My father was a farmer and a laborer, not that farming wasn't labor. He was strong and I loved to be with him; it was a way I escaped the taunts of my brother and sister. He taught me by example and with work, but most of all he had confidence in my abilities. I could run faster than any of my cousins. I could ride my pony faster, a pony that could jump the fences with ease.

My dad had so much confidence in my running he would say to me, "I'm not going to worry about you in the pasture; you can outrun the bull." When we would be out picking berries in the woods, he would say, "I'm not going to worry about you because you can move faster than a rattlesnake can strike." At the same time he would teach me about the snakes, the wildlife, the woods, the waters and the pastures.

I could ask questions and get answers. He taught me to look for answers, new ways, improved ways, to be better. I now realize that he was brilliant in mathematics with a third-grade education. He taught me about numbers; I would sit mesmerized at our kitchen table as he manipulated numbers. Consequently, I grew up believing I could do math, or anything for that matter. I loved math.

My mother was an amazing woman. She was tall, stately, and beautiful. She wanted to get an education but was sent to La Crosse, Wisconsin, to work for a family that owned a brewery. But she never lost that desire for education. Even when I was in high school, she went to night classes to study typing and shorthand.

Mother was a religious person. We went to church and Sunday school, prayer meeting, youth group, or any other activity that came along in the church. She had the most fantastic way of making her points, saying something that was indisputable. She had a German saying or a proverb for every situation. Often it was short, but it was always to the point.

When I went to college, my father borrowed the first $50 that I used. From that point forward, mother would always have my $28 for tuition each quarter of my first two years and $32 during the last two years. She sold berries in the summer, cottage cheese, or whatever she might be able to sell to earn a few pennies for my tuition; somehow, she managed to have the money. Food, lodging, and incidentals were my responsibility.

I have given you this picture of my parents and my situation because it doesn't seem like the road map that would lead to the wonderful professional career that I have had—deanships and professorial appointments at major universities, degrees and awards. But as I have come to know, we are all given everything that we need when we are born. Everything is right and everything that we need is available to us if we ask and believe.

THE PLENTIFUL UNIVERSE

That is the *secret*. The Universe is a plentiful place. There isn't a shortage of anything. It does seem so at times, and shortages may come into our lives. They exist when we believe that they exist. Because we believe they exist, they come into our lives.

While I was packing pickles in jars, picking berries, or hoeing my potato field, I had plenty of time to dream, to vision the places I could go, the things that I would be able to do. I could be anywhere and be anything in what Walt Disney would call "Imagineering." I was thinking, and therefore, asking.

I'm quite certain that if anyone saw me day after day in the potato field that I planted one summer to earn a little money, they would not have visualized me in a doctoral program at UCLA, as graduate dean in the College of Education at the University of Cincinnati, or Dean of Education at Oregon State University. As the beads of perspiration rolled off of my body in the hot summer Iowa sun, I sensed my future could be what I wanted it to be. What was the *secret* of my dreams and expectations?

SIGNPOSTS OF OPPORTUNITY

I had so many signposts of opportunity along the way.

As a student, when I worked for the superintendent in my small high school during the Great Depression, I kept the words of a sign in his office on the front burner of my mind. It said "There is always room at the top." No matter how many times that I heard how bad things were, how difficult it was to get a job, how long the food lines were, even how it felt to be hungry, I knew that there was room at the top and that meant opportunity all the way up the ladder.

My basketball coach, math teacher and friend wrote in my freshman memory book: "To one who is at home in all lands and ages and has lost herself in generous enthusiasm plus cooperation with others for common ends. It is my sincere hope that you will carry the keys of the world's library in your pocket and feel its resources behind you in whatever task you undertake."

Eddie Albertson was an inspiration, a friend, a mentor, a pusher, a person who expected me to be excellent at whatever I did. When we played our games of H-O-R-S-E at basketball practice, he expected me to win some of those games. He loaned me advanced math books for the summer. He encouraged me with a note during the summer while he was away playing baseball. I had other wonderful teachers in elementary and high school, but none knew how to unlock the joy and amazement of my physical and mental gifts the way Mr. Albertson did. Thank you, Coach. You helped me lay many bricks on my road of the future. What was your secret?

When I graduated, I doubt that many in my town of 1,321 population expected me to go to college, but my teachers were not surprised when I enrolled at Iowa State Teachers College. Although my parents said little about college, I don't think that they were surprised either. I knew I had to go; I expected it of me.

College was interesting. I soon found that I had to pursue two paths of learning: one to do what was required to get the grades and the other to find and capture the learning that I needed as a person. I also learned quickly that I needed to disregard the advice and counsel from those persons who placed limitations on me. How dare they be so foolish? I was the only one who could place personal limitations. I alone was in charge of my thoughts and beliefs about what I could and couldn't accomplish.

Keeping that focus was not always easy. I looked around and as I interacted with people, I wondered: Was I really a fit? My father was a laborer; my parents had little education although they were very bright. I had to work to eat; I didn't know what a country club was; and I didn't know how few clothes I had until other students complained about the size of their closet. I almost started blaming my parents for all the "things" other students had that I didn't. But then I remembered the gifts they had given me that could not be purchased. Yes, I had been given everything that I needed.

THE LADY

Along the way in college, I had remarkable professors. The best teacher was Doris White, a physical education professor. She knew the power of positive thinking and acting; she knew the power of expectation. She knew the power of faith in another human being, the greatness of service, and the satisfaction gained from arduous tasks and successful performance.

She modeled compassion and love, truth and integrity. She modeled the universal Law of Attraction. She never used the phrase or told us that was what it was, but she taught us to ask, believe, and you will receive. She taught us to always ask for the behavior we wanted, to never tell students what we didn't want. I marvel at what she taught us without labels. I have come to understand the magnitude of this woman and her considerable influence on our lives.

You must know this story about this lady. As a sophomore in college, I decided I needed to get my teeth straightened. I boldly went to a dentist and asked him to do it with the proviso that I would pay what I could and would definitely finish the payments when I started teaching, which was then over two years away. He agreed and I had braces. They fit inside my teeth, which caused me to lisp painfully and noticeably. I bravely went to all my professors with my plight; I asked if they would just call on me when I volunteered because that would be the time that I could speak without too much embarrassment.

They all agreed to "help me." That is, until I came to Miss White. We were standing next to the steps on the third floor of the women's gymnasium when I explained my dilemma. She looked at me with her wonderful smile and cheerfully said, "Miss Boltz, I will be happy to help you; I will call on you when I think you will get the most practice saying the words that are difficult for you."

I was angry. Didn't she care? Didn't she understand? She knew she would have plenty of times to give me practice since I was in her kinesiology class as well as several theory and activity classes. Imagine the opportunity she had to "help" me with all the sounds in the names of the bones, muscles, and nerves. She kept her word. When I finished the quarter, I realized that she was the only one who really "helped" me. I was able to speak clearly and the embarrassment was gone. She had the courage to give me what I needed and had asked for. Thank you, Miss White, for the incredible learning.

Through all the experiences, I learned to ask, I learned to believe, I learned to expect and to be grateful when I received what I asked for. That is the *secret*. It is the great law of the universe, the Law of Attraction. I was attracting into my life everything that was happening. I knew, but I had no name for "it" at that time.

And then I graduated, a twenty year old excited educator with a job in hand. Would I remember the evidence in my life that I had to know what I wanted, to vision it, and ask for what I wanted? Would I remember that the response would be to what I was thinking? Would I remember that I was the tower transmitting thoughts?

Would I remember and understand and be able to pass on the secrets of enchanting learning places?

CHAPTER 2

AN ENCHANTED PLACE

Would I remember the enchantment of my learning places? Yes.
The memories were etched in my being.

The love and joy of my enchanting learning places were imprinted
on my soul. As a teacher, I would remember that I had the opportunity to create places of enchantment every day. What other profession can experience the constant joy of creating places of enchantment, magic kingdoms for minds that yearn to learn, and beings that
want to be happy and be able to smile? We look for enchantment.
We look for adventure. We travel the world to see the miracles that
have been wrought in architecture and art. We marvel at the beauty
of nature.

Strange how we are always looking outside of ourselves. Interesting
that we continue to look for the greener pastures. It is sad that so
many of us feel our jobs are boring and dull. We get up at the same
time each day, go through the same motions each day, and expect
that the day's happenings will be like the day before and the day
after. Often our great chance passes us by.

Perhaps it was a blessing that during most of my "school years" I
was monetarily poor. I never sought to buy enchantment. But why
would I want to? My world was full of incredible happenings and
things. The yellow fuzz on my ducklings was softer than any fabric
I could have found anywhere in the world. The nettles stung with
such strength that I knew nature was not an accident.

What an amazing world! The birds that sang and the chorus that was created by the many different birds and songs as I walked through the woods or, just listened most anywhere, told me that I was living nature's harmony at its best. Watching the grain grow from the planting to the golden harvest was full of mystery and glory. And the *Farmer's Almanac* was somewhere close by for me to read. Was it too early to plant peas? Was it the right time to plant the second or even third batch of radishes and lettuce seeds so we could have fresh vegetables until that first visit of Jack Frost in the fall?

Have you ever looked closely at an apple blossom? How can such a beautiful thing wither and lose its beauty only to produce that magnificent red, yellow or green apple in the fall? The tadpoles to frogs, the caterpillar to butterfly, the eggs in the incubator to wonderful furry little chickens – all were magic to watch. Have you ever watched a little chicken trying to get out of its shell? How could you not be filled with questions? How could you miss the enchantment of science? Why does my granddaughter not like "school" science but reads and talks about science in its true form with interest?

I sat mesmerized as I listened to my mom and dad talk of the pack of wolves following them as they traveled by horse and buggy from one farmhouse to another in North Dakota. I looked at the Indian mounds that exist in Iowa and Wisconsin and wondered what the lives were of those who lived then. I talked with the Indian family next door to our farm. I learned and respected.

History was everywhere around me; it was evident when I talked to my uncle who fought in the Spanish American War, when I listened to my grandfather who came to America with his knapsack and little more, when I rode in our first Model T Ford, when I read my history and geography books. Surrounding me was the enchantment of history.

Numbers always intrigued me. I think most of the wonder came because of my dad. Perhaps I was talking to him about the homework in math; I don't remember exactly. I don't think I would have been complaining because I loved school so much. Dad would see me doing math and he would sit or very quietly come out with some profound statement. One that influenced me in my love of math was: "Honey, numbers are just like people; you do certain things with them or treat them in certain ways and they respond in certain ways."

I would be adding columns of numbers and he would sit down; he would ask me to write a big column of numbers as wide or deep as I chose. Then he would take his finger and go down the columns, no matter how many, and write the answer. How could I not be enchanted with numbers? And I know that I have never really gotten to the most enchanting numbers, those in quantum physics and those in the uncertainty principles of Heisenberg. Where is the enchantment of math today for most of our students? How can my granddaughter be so good at math and still dislike it? What happened in "school math" that killed the enchantment?

How can kids love sports, and hate PE? How can they sing and dance and listen to music with such joy and hate their music class? What happened to the storyteller, the artist of kindergarten who doesn't like to write by the third grade, who is afraid to do art by the sixth grade?

My little country school house was such an enchanting place. When

I went there, I was still in the primary grades, doing second- and third-grade work officially. But I guess nobody made that specific because I just did what I wanted and was able to do. If something interesting was happening in an upper grade, I would listen and do the work, or I would go sit with someone in that grade and participate.

It was wonderful. Nobody told me I couldn't do the work, that it wasn't my grade, or to get busy and do my own work. No one made me do stuff I already knew how to do, or even work that I had no reason to want to do. Wouldn't you think that was an enchanting place? I did.

MIRACLES BY THE MINUTE

Educators are in a profession that offers miracles every minute of the day, opportunities to create enchanting places for learning. It depends greatly on how we view our jobs. We should be able to answer anyone who asks us the question, "Why are you here; why are you a teacher?" We must be able to say that we are teaching because it is what we want to do and where we are is the only place that we want to be. Then we will be able to multiply "opportunity" times the number of interactions that we have in a day and we can experience the miraculous nature of the day that we can have. But we have to believe that we live in a world of energy and wonderful universal laws that allow for a life of miracles in the classroom.

What happens every day is not the mystery that we make it to be, nor is it a hodgepodge of random happenings. All the action and interactions happen in accordance with universal laws. Scientists know, and teachers above all other workers, should want to know what science knows. One thing quantum physicists have given us is that energy flows around us and among us at all times. We are not working in space that is empty and devoid of consciousness. Energy vibrates within us and around us.

When my classrooms were set up, I always tried to position furniture in ways that allowed as many people as possible to see each other rather than the back of someone. It always seemed prudent to try for as much interaction as possible. My explanations at times must have seemed strange because I did not have the words to explain so many of the concepts that I knew if only intuitively. I always explained that any space that we had that existed to our eyes as empty space—that is devoid of furniture and students—was not really empty space, but was filled with the energy that we brought.

I always insisted that only positive energy be brought into the room. Any negative thought or expression was to be left at the door. As a result, our time together was positive and allowed everyone the opportunity to participate and grow. It became a safe place. A safe environment allows all to become a part of a learning community, a place where the creativity can blossom. It is a place where learners are free to be a part of creating an enchanting learning place.

TIMELESS

This is an idea that is timeless; it is not new science. We all know it consciously or intuitively. When our classrooms are filled with positive energy, they become happy, productive places. Places of enchantment are created with the energy that flows in and around us. This energy and consciousness are in perpetual motion.

Because it is invisible to the human eye should not make it less believable. What we "see" as solid objects quantum physicists have discovered are made up of vibrating strings of energy. Scientists believe that we determine the outcome of our experiences by what we do with our consciousness and energy. A small shift in energy has the possibility of creating large differences and far-reaching changes in our reality.

When I think about the many authors who have explained this concept in slightly different words, one thing always is the end concept. The Universe/Source/God or whatever word helps you to understand, the idea is that powerful energy exists. There is no end; there is no shortage. There is no rationing to the just or the unjust; there is just this abundant powerful energetic world. It is ever present and available.

There is more than enough for everyone. If I have eminent success, it does not diminish the possibility for someone else. If I gain eminent wealth or fame, it does not diminish the possibility for others. This energy source is not a pie or a finite amount of something. The more of this energy that we use in either positive or negative ways, the more we receive.

We live in a world of unlimited potential and possibilities. We have heard this and we have iterated statements that would indicate that is what we believe.

"You can be anything you want to be."
"Think big."
"Follow your dreams; dreams can come true."

WHEN THE STUDENT IS READY

Over the many years of my career—yes, my entire life experience—I have been amazed to find the "lessons of life" everywhere I turn. There is a Zen saying that "when the student is ready, the teacher appears." The teacher has appeared so many times when it seemed I needed a lesson, an insight, an understanding. So many have appeared in books that have come my way. One of these that carries such an abundance of insight into our jobs as teachers and learners is the story of *Jonathan Livingston Seagull*, by Richard Bach.

Jonathan is a young seagull that insists on being the seagull he was meant to be. He keeps flying his own patterns and believes that there is more to life than flying the same patterns the other gulls fly looking for scraps and garbage on the beaches. The great ocean and the horizon draw him out farther to explore and realize the gifts that he has been given.

When Jonathan's mother kept asking him why it was so hard for him to be like the rest of the flock, I am reminded of the times, too numerous to count, that I have heard similar comments from teachers, parents, counselors, administrators, and others. "Why can't you just be like the others? Why can't you use the writing prompts that all the others use? I taught you how to solve the math problem. Why do you have to solve it your way? Do you think you are a mathematical genius or something? Your picture looks different; why are your hills purple?"

As the teacher tries to get the "gulls" to conform, the works that are different become crumpled papers in the "round file" and the wings are clipped.

But the story of Jonathan gives hope. Jonathan continued his exploration of flight at night and in daylight. He was fully aware that gulls didn't fly at night, but he found it beautiful. He learned to do a snap roll and the loop, the inverted spin, and much more. When Jonathan joined the flock on the beach one night, he flew a loop to landing and a snap roll before touchdown.

Jonathan was elated and thought the flock would be "wild with joy." He was showing them how much more there was to living than their routine of going back and forth to the fishing boats. Jonathan was proving that there was more to life than that. They could be intelligent and skillful gulls. They could be free.

How often I have seen the little ones come into kindergarten filled with the joy of a Jonathan, filled with expectations of new things, energized with excitement to learn. So often they find that the safest road is to "do and be what is expected." Just as Jonathan is called before the Council Gathering, so too are little newcomers to the educational system called before the Authority. Like Jonathan, they are told that they have violated the rules and are not acting responsibly. "You must learn to be responsible," they are told.

Just as our learners come to us as sons and daughters of life's longing for itself, as beings trying to tread the paths of fulfillment and the roads of their potential, Jonathan felt his responsibility was to find and follow the higher purpose of life, to journey in the skies of his potential and be who he was meant to be.

BEYOND THE BEACHES

My memory of my first reading of *Jonathan Livingston Seagull* was one of astonishment. How could an author capture so much of what I had felt in some of my educational experiences when people tried to keep me on the beach looking for scraps? I marveled at the feeling of freedom I had as I followed Jonathan into the skies way beyond the beach.

I look back and I wonder. Why was I always so willing to live on the edge? Why was I constantly trying to learn new things, try things I hadn't tried before, begin big projects? I looked forward to each new day and thought it would bring surprise, joy, and amazement. The scraps on the beach were not sufficient. The sunset got more interesting each day and at night the moon held ever more mystery and wonderment. As with Jonathan, seeing the beauty of the horizon and the night skies was so exhilarating for me.

I still wonder why learning is so tedious and uninteresting for so many I see.

The joy of Jonathan's learning courses through my veins as I re-read his story. The joy of my own learning is the greatest wonderment of all. It is as impossible for me as it was for Jonathan to imagine days without curious interaction with everything I know and don't know. As with Jonathan, it has always been true—in school, out of school, in the city, on the farm, with others, alone, with a book, without a book, speaking or listening, running or walking, swimming or sleeping—just being.

Jonathan had a different vision than the other gulls. How horrible and humiliating for the flock. But when you embark upon a vision of your world that is limitless you fly high and experience the tantalizing tastes and smells and touch of each new day's learning. Why were the highs so high, the struggles so great when interference reared its ugly head? Joy and ecstasy were high; tears so salty. And when someone would try to throw water on the fire of my spirit or close the damper on my draft of energy, it was faith, boundless parameter of aid from outside me that rescued me.

My golden days of summer as a child had some idling time. It was then that I could dream and be in those dreams. It was then that I could look up at the sun and the stars and the moon and be in awe about it all. What were they? Where were they in space and time? It was then that I could wonder about me. As I lay on the grass I could learn to run faster, climb farther, read and write without paper and books. It was then that I started to realize the lack of boundaries to all the things that had been given boundaries. I could be on the edge and not fall off.

Samuel Taylor Coleridge's poem describes that state.

What if you slept,
And what if, in your sleep you dreamed,
And what if in your dream you went to heaven.

And there you plucked a strange and wonderful flower?
And what if, when you awoke
You had the flower in your hand?
What then?

Yes, what then?

My world was not flat or round; it could be what I needed it to be. It didn't even have to be what others said it was or wanted it to be or even insisted it was. It was at these times when the Mississippi River could be dark and ominous or lively or angry or quiet; it only mattered what I made it. I could build the castles of my future of whatever I pleased. I could fashion the tapestries of my dreams and when they were woven, I could climb aboard and fly away.

And so the days of summer were followed by the gold and yellow and red leaves of fall, and of climbing trees and climbing the ladders within. Soon the leaves would turn brown and start falling to the ground. What a great model for change. The leaves fall, the snows come, and even the water in the river changes to ice. It made it easy to understand change and the interconnectedness of everything.

AND THEN…

And then I learned to teach. I studied hard; I listened patiently; I wrote dutifully. I graduated promptly with my credentials.

But I graduated also with much of my vision of learning intact. Yes, I memorized all of the stuff on the unending tables in my biology classes—plants and animals. Show it to me, and I could name it. But I never taught biology like that. Biology was more interesting than that; I would try to make it so. When I asked students to create, I meant for them to do so.

Somehow, my two-track personal education system—one track to get the grade, and the other to gain the knowledge that was important for me—saved me from becoming what I was supposed to become according to the rules of academia. And I must give credit to those teachers and professors who allowed me to fly beyond the shore.

OUR GREATEST GIFTS

Flying beyond the shore to become everything that our potential demands is our greatest gift to ourselves. Being the best that we can be is our greatest gift to others.

Gibran's statement about children from *The Prophet* has been cited many times; I have read it to hundreds of teachers. It needs to be given here:

> These children are not your children,
> They are the sons and daughters of Life's longing for itself.
> They come through you, but not from you.
> And though they are with you yet they belong not to you
> You may give them your love but not your thoughts,
> For they have their own thoughts.
> You may house their bodies but not their souls
> For their souls dwell in the house of tomorrow,
> Which you cannot visit, not even in your dreams.
> You may strive to be like them,
> But seek not to make them like you.

The next task is allowing others to be who they must be and learning to control what you do in your interactions with them to be what you need to be rather than trying to control who they are or even who they will become. Your model will speak louder than millions of words.

My granddaughter loves to play with little people and little animals; they are Hasbro toys from The Littlest Pet. We were talking one day about writing. She asked if she had to write from some of the prompts. Could she write her own stories? She proceeded to tell me stories that she had created with her little folk. For forty-five minutes she continued with one story after another. She had, in fact, told me enough stories for a chapter book. I was amazed and sat transfixed as she related one story after the other, each a captivating tale.

She explained that she had not told anyone about her thoughts because she was afraid they would make fun of her for wanting to "play" with the Littlest Pet toys. She felt they would want her "to grow up." Her fear was that they might think she should "grow out of it," and that they would not want her to play with little girl things. I explained that all creative folks have tools and props and a place where they create. Artists use crayons and pencils and paints; so do small children.

Our solution was to make a place, a studio, where she could go with her Littlest Pets to create her tapestries of thought, her ideas put to paper, or tape if she preferred. The smile of joy and the demeanor of relief were monumental. It was a way to make her feel comfortable about something that was important and fun and which produced very creative anecdotal happenings. Then the thought popped up about what would Mommy and Daddy think? I assured her they would be very happy when they read her writing.

The sadness I felt that a child should have to worry about being creative was not a new feeling for me. I had experienced it so many times before in my career. Whether it was a small child hesitant about the worthiness of an idea or a doctoral student asking to do original research, it was always the same. The hesitancy about sharing something outside the box always presents itself in the same way. Others might not find it worthy. Lest I forget, I keep a saying framed on my office wall: "Only those who see the invisible can do the impossible."

We must constantly remind our learners of their potential. We must remind them that they do not have to follow the flock; they do not have to be bound by the limitations that others place on them. They can fly freely. They are not confined to the garbage on the shore or to the flights back and forth to the ships. The sky is theirs.

It is no different for us. We must constantly remind ourselves that these children, learners of any age, are not our children. They are the sons and daughters of life's longing for itself. From little toe to last hair, they are the unlimited idea of freedom and image of our Creator, the Great Source, and their whole body from little toe to last hair is nothing more than their thought itself. How do we serve this incredible being, rather than try to fix it or try to make it what we think it should be rather than what it needs to become, life's longing for itself?

Jonathan refused to leave his places of enchantment—the night sky and the sky beyond the beaches. We must create places of enchantment that our learners will not want to leave. We must be certain that we are not limiting their flying to the beaches or to flight patterns that are designed to pick up the garbage from the ships that pass by.

If I were teaching now, I would examine my day to make certain that my students were free to do snap-rolls and dives and all manner of self-realizing patterns of flight. I would urge them to find the flight patterns that would take them to the realm of all that they could be. They will find those patterns in places of enchantment.

For a period of a week, as I finished each day, I would stop for a few moments and journal ways that might have increased the horizon, placed fewer limitation on students, or increased their ability to seek greater horizons, greater freedom to pursue new ideas or skills. I would share this with students the next day and ask for their input. I would use the exercise to work with parents as well as teachers or other school personnel.

I would be in a state of exploration for new horizons. I would stretch my mind and the minds of my students, knowing that once stretched, they could never return to their original shapes. Together we would look for new places to fly, for new patterns of flight, and for new horizons.

CHAPTER 3

THE DIFFERENCE

What is the difference between the great learning environments, the places of enchantment and those that diminish the joy and hinder the learning? What's the difference between the room that students enter with a smile and the room that students enter with a frown and heavy heart? How can it be that a student, the same student, can be a happy learner in one and a reluctant, recalcitrant non-learner in the next room the next hour? Is it possible that a student can love the second grade and be a "model student" there and go to the third grade and be a "horrible mess"? Yes, we can say that there are inter-vening circumstances that caused the differences.

But I would like to propose that the differences lie mainly with the teacher. I would like to suggest that the teacher attracts and is the dominant factor for the behavior that is present. Yes, there are students who are also sending out vibrations. Indeed, they do have their own thoughts. We might ask the question, "What good would it do to think good thoughts about bad behavior?" The science of thought tells us that our thoughts change the behavior of those around us. The better and the more positive our thoughts, the more things im-prove for us and those around us.

A law in the universe says, "Like attracts like," or that which is like itself is drawn. I have watched students come to school as new students and by the end of the first day or shortly thereafter, the new student will have chosen a set of acquaintances or friends. As a counselor in high school, I saw this happen without exception. We knew by the end of a very short time what the student would be like.

Sometimes we would change teachers or change classes to mitigate potential difficult circumstances. For centuries we have said, "Birds of a feather flock together."

Have you ever started the day feeling unhappy or sad, and found matters to get worse and worse as the day progressed? How many times have you said, "Today, I should have stayed in bed." I have heard that many times from teachers. And their day has gone the way of the first few minutes—unless they understand the Law of Attraction. If they understand that they can change the circumstances because they are the thinker of the thoughts, they can change their day. They can feel better by the end of the day rather than worse.

"Oh, I wish I didn't have this class the first period in the morning! It ruins my whole day." The Law of Attraction will bring exactly what is asked for and believed. The general reaction is, "You certainly don't think that I asked my class to be that way. I would love it if they would turn in to a good class." Yes, the Law of Attraction is certain. It knows that you are talking about the class behaving a certain way, being a certain way. It will give it to you whether or not you want it. It doesn't discriminate between what you want or don't want. It gives you what you ask for—what your thoughts are. If you want the class to be different, you must ask for the behavior you want, believe that it will happen, and sit back and watch it happen.

Coming to school not feeling well is certain to turn into something more than not feeling well by the time you have told several people you don't feel well. By the end of the day you will feel the way your day went—lousy.

LOOKING BACK

Once we understand the Law of Attraction, we can look back and see that it has been in action in our lives, including our teaching lives. We have received what we have been asking for (what we have been thinking) whether we wanted it or not.

When I was a freshman in college, I worked in a private home where I received my room and board. All of my classes had to be taken in the morning; the afternoons and evenings were kept free to work for the family. In order to pursue a double major, double minor program of studies in my sophomore year, I needed to live close to campus and have my afternoons for classes; I knew that I could not continue to work for my board and room for a family that gave me only mornings for school. I had money enough for my room but needed a source for my meals.

I decided the best place was to work where there was food. Mack's Café was a popular eatery close to campus and my room, which was just off campus. I boldly asked the owner for a job. He politely told me the jobs were all filled. I explained that I needed the job so I could eat. I sat down and told him that I would wait. I recall the strange, quizzical look on his face. There was a moment of silence as he continued to look at me and I at him. It seemed like an eternity, but in reality it was a very short time until he said with a knowing smile, "Well, put on an apron and get to work." ASK, BELIEVE, AND RECEIVE. That is the Law of Attraction at work in our lives. It's an incredible blessing or curse. As we will! But I am certain that it is certain and always is the same

I have told the story many times and have experienced many different responses. Wow, what courage. How did you have such courage at such a young age? Why didn't you walk away when he told you there were no jobs left? How did an unknown student like you get a job there? I knew they hired the popular men and women on campus. I sensed one thing: I could not get a job if I didn't ask, and if I didn't expect to be hired why would I expect anyone else to hire me? Somehow I knew! But now I know what to call the force I felt. It's the Law of Attraction.

Whatever you are giving your attention to causes you to emit a vibration, and the vibrations that you offer equal your asking, which equals your point of attraction. Consequently, if you are thinking predominantly about the things that you desire, your life experience reflects those things. In the same way, if you are predominantly thinking about what you do not want, your life experience reflects those things. Worrying is using your imagination to create something you do not want. You cannot desire something, predominantly focus on the absence of it, and expect to receive it. So it is with our classrooms.

THE INVITATION

Nothing can occur in your life experience without your invitation of it through your thought. Every thought that you give your attention to expands and becomes a bigger part of your vibrational mix. Whether it is a thought of something you want or a thought of something you do not want, your attention to it invites it into your experience. Your focus is the attention; your attention is the invitation. Think about what this means in your classroom.

Your thoughts equal your point of attraction, and the way that you feel indicates your level of allowing or resisting. It is not possible for you to consistently feel positive emotion about something and have it turn out badly. Nor is it possible for you to consistently feel bad about something and have it turn out well. You can tell by the way you feel whether you are, in this moment, helping or hindering. As you ponder this, think about specific examples from a class that was special—especially good or especially challenging.

Distinguishing between the actual thought of what you want, compared to the thought of its absence, is difficult. But distinguishing between your emotional response to your thought of your desire, and your emotional response to your thought of the absence of your desire, is a very easy thing to do. When you are fully focused upon your desire, you feel wonderful. And when you focus upon the absence of something you truly want, you feel awful. Once you begin to understand the correlation between what you are thinking, what you are feeling, and what you are receiving, you have it. You have the secret to a place of enchantment.

Your emotions do not create, but they do indicate what you are currently attracting. Pay attention to the way you feel. Deliberately choose thoughts about everything that feel good to you when you make them.

We always hold the power and control of our life experience. The only reason that we could ever experience something other than what we desire is because we are giving the majority of our attention to something other than what we want. We get what we think about whether we want it or not. So it is in our classrooms.

If we have the ability to imagine it or even to think about it, this Universe has the ability and the resources to deliver it fully to us. Once we understand the Law of Attraction, we can look back and see that it has been in action in our lives, most certainly in our teaching and learning lives. We have received what we have been asking for (what we have been thinking) whether we wanted it or not.

Remember, it is everywhere around us and with us. It governs all persons the same whether we choose to understand it or not. It is available to us for use in our private and public lives, in our professional lives, and in our classrooms. It is available to help us create places of enchantment or...

As you react to the ideas in this chapter, be as concrete as you can about what you're thinking, about the concepts and ideas. Relate them to your most recent teaching and learning experiences.

CHAPTER 4

BELIEVING IS SEEING

One day I was visiting my son who was teaching physical education to "special kids." They were special education first-grade children who perhaps could profit from some special kinesthetic activities. He asked if I would observe Jimmy (not his name) as he bounced a ball up and down the playfield. I asked what I was looking for. He said, "Just tell me what you see."

Jimmy bounced the ball easily with either hand, shifted the ball from one hand to the other, did interesting things with his feet—he skipped, hopped, ran slowly, ran swiftly—made the whole exercise into his very own game. He was full of joy and creativity. And he certainly showed excellent physical abilities. It was obvious that he was thinking of ways to add interest to his activity.

When the class was over my son said, "Well, what do you think?" I told him that I thought Jimmy showed many signs of being a gifted child. I shared what I observed. My son told me that he felt the same way, but was puzzled why the child was there. The teacher had asked him to give her a report on the child; she had suggested that he had "problems and was slow."

We talked about how to report to the teacher about our observations. I suggested that he tell the teacher that we thought the child might be gifted. Perhaps the teacher could look for clues to help him work with the child. He told the teacher what a joy the child was and how wonderfully he responded to instructions and suggestions. Working with him was fun and he looked forward to more opportunities.

A couple of weeks later, I asked my son how Jimmy was doing. He told me that he had not had Jimmy in his groups again. When he asked the teacher where Jimmy was, she said she thought that his observations were correct; he did appear to be gifted. How does a teacher with one set of observations from someone go from thinking a child is retarded or slow to gifted? By changing what she believed about the child. BELIEVING IS SEEING!! She saw what she believed.

THE UNIVERSE IN REVERSE

We have generally been taught that. "Seeing is believing." "Show me and I'll believe it." "I'm from Missouri, the show-me state."

Unfortunately, we have the universe in reverse.

The most conclusive proof for this that I can offer is from the research, hard data-driven research. It is too easy to throw the idea away by counting it as unfounded, a fad, or something out of the "New Age" stuff. It is too important to the future of all of our learners and other contacts in our lives to not understand these scientific findings. We dismiss what we see as happenstance or unusual when it doesn't fit our paradigm. This is a concept that when practiced, changes everything. It is a 180 degree turn.

As a former biology teacher, I know the magnitude of the change. I was programmed to believe, as were you, that life was controlled by genes. It is understandable why the works of the scientists who proposed otherwise were dismissed. The paradigm shift was just too great to embrace. Reasons were given to try to discredit the research by suggesting that the data were irrelevant, the research was not done correctly, protocols were not followed, or that the sample was insufficient. In many cases it was criticized as just bad research. In truth, the research outcomes conflicted with what was "already known and accepted."

WE WAIT

Scientists who were changing the landscape of cell biology could not get their research published. They could not be heard in the "important" circles of science nor found in the chronicles of scientific journals. But that is the unfortunate nature of all sacred science kept in the annals and cubicles of "Revered Ones." It is why as graduate dean in a well-known university I saw incredibly gifted students leave; they could not pursue their dreams and creativeness. They could only pursue the research interests of the professors in charge.

It is why we wait so long for the incredible findings to creep into our lives.

We cannot afford to let new and life changing research done on the brain to languish on the shelves of the unbelieving because it messes up their tidy world. We cannot wait for them to believe. We have each generation of students coming before us each day. It is time for new models; a Model T Ford in a space ship age is not acceptable.

The research is fascinating. It has not been easily accepted because it flies in the face of some fully entrenched beliefs. But, as educators, we dare not be wrong on this one. Of the many books that I have read on the subject, the one from my perspective that comes

47

the closest to helping us understand the science, even by its title, is The Biology of Belief.

Dr. Bruce Lipton puts the research and concepts together in ways that are easy to understand and apply to our learning and teaching. Lipton describes the life-changing moments as he saw his research on how cells control their physiology and behavior. He realized that a cell's life was controlled by the physical and energy environment and not by its genetic makeup, its genes.

The amazing thing is that if one cell can be controlled by awareness of its environment, then the 50 trillion cells that make up a human being are likewise controlled by their environment and not by their genes. This is the 180-degree turn.

As we learn about the magic of the cells, we gradually shed the old Darwinian shell of survival of the fittest and start to don a new mantle—one that reflects the cooperative nature of the 50 trillion individual cells that make up each one of us. The lesson of the cells is momentous. These trillions of cells live together harmoniously to survive. When the harmony is not there, there is disease and trauma.

The lesson of harmony and peace is there for us to see and copy in our lives and in our classrooms. We can learn that we are not what our "genes make us." We have control. Our thinking produces our environment. and as teachers we craft the environment for our students. We believe, we think; we act. Our beliefs control our thinking and, therefore, our lives.

As I have sat in the lunchroom or in the teachers room, I have heard the argument about a learner's environment or her genetic background, usually some kind or unkind comments about her relatives. How do you expect Susie to do anything! Just look where she comes from. And, of course, with that comment the dodge continues. It removes the responsibility of both parties, teacher and student, from the real potential for a different way to live.

The scientific research of the last short while shows us that our genes do not control our biology. It is the environment in which the cells exist that controls. The research of the New Biology has profound implications for our lives and our professional behavior.

When we become victims of our biology, we live our lives with the conviction that what happens just happens; we were born that way. When you transfer that Darwinian premise to the classroom, victimization sets in. What do you expect me to do with this bunch? What can they do? Look who their parents are. This is tragic for the learning environment. It is as poisonous to the learning community in that space as a poison in a body is to the community of cells.

As a biology student, I was taught with certainty that the nucleus of the cell was the controlling factor, the mother-board of control. Then I learned that it is not the gene-carrying nucleus that programs the cell, but rather it is the cell's membrane's receptors where the data are entered into the cell. It is there that the effector proteins process the environmental information that comes in. This is a huge paradigm shift. We do not have to be victims; we can edit the data that come in. Our bio-computers are ready and able. We can monitor the data.

We must understand that we are dealing with energy, the energy as known in quantum physics. Just as most have ignored the role of energy in our lives—the manifestation of health and disease—so have most ignored the role of energy in our classrooms. I have known for most of my educational career that my classroom or any space in which I was working was not just made of the "solid objects" like the chairs and the students; it was in fact made up of energy. This requires another huge paradigm shift in our thinking.

We must shed the Newtonian physics and embrace the principles of quantum physics. During my tenure at Oregon State, I invited Fritjof Capra, a physicist, to our campus to work with the science teachers and science educators of the state and our university. One of the presentations that he did was a comparison of the ideas of quantum physics with Eastern mysticism. As he overlaid one idea on the other, one could see the sameness, the congruence of his illustrations.

We must come to understand what philosophers and Eastern mysticism have understood about energy fields. We must come to understand what quantum physics knows about energy fields.

When I was directing Upward Bound, I was amazed at the special talents of the Native American students with whom I had the pleasure of working. No matter what the tribal affiliation, each student was a systems thinker. Each looked at his/her world in a holistic manner. They talked of the wholeness—their inability to separate parts of the universe. They spoke of the parts as being one. All things were interdependent.

They taught me that energy and matter are intertwined, that the mind and body are bound together. Somehow, no matter what the science, we still try to separate mind and body, particularly in medicine and education. We have plenty of evidence that harnessing the energy, the power of the mind, is extremely potent. Energy—thought—is immensely powerful.

THOUGHTS—OUR MIND'S ENERGY

Our thoughts, our mind's energy, are precious. They directly exercise control of the physical brain and, therefore, our behavior. For those of us who spend our lives with our most precious commodity, our young people, it is imperative that we understand these principles. We must learn to monitor our thoughts because we get what we think about. Remember, we get what we ask for whether or not we want it. Whatever you are thinking about, you are attracting to you. When you think that Jimmy is retarded, (perhaps there is a note in the cum folder) you transmit that to Jimmy and to everyone you meet or anyone in your presence.

You are a transmitter of vibrations of energy. Those vibrations are out there. But you ask how can a teacher change that fact? She can do it with a simple process over which she has total control. She is the thinker of her thoughts and, she can be the changer of her thoughts. It seems so amazing, and it is. It seems so easy, and it is. It seems so miraculous, and it is. We are the thinkers of our thoughts and we can be the changers of our thoughts.

Why, you ask, does it not happen more? I believe that educators have been putting the science of thought, the science of energy vibrations, and the universal Law of Attraction in the category of "New Age" stuff. We may read the theory of observer-created reality, which tells us that intention and consciousness are at work and are real forces, but we don't or can't use the information. This is true of our personal lives as well as our educator lives. Everything we do, we first think. Everything exists in our consciousness first.

Last Sunday morning as I was getting ready for church, I was listening to a news program that has a health segment. A research study about peanut allergies was discussed. The study was done in two countries. In one, there was no worry about pregnant mothers who ate peanuts passing along an allergic reaction to their children. In the other country, there was a belief that if pregnant mothers did not eat peanuts and the baby wasn't exposed to peanuts for a period of time, the child would have a much better chance of not being allergic to peanuts. The study showed that the children of the mothers who were trying to protect their children from the allergy were far more prone to peanut allergy than the mothers who did not believe there would be a problem with allergies to peanuts.

The doctor reporting the study found this to be fascinating and wondered why this was the case. It is, to me, an excellent example of believing is seeing. The populations were similar and the genes may have been carrying disparate knowledge/beliefs about peanut allergies, but the large difference was in what they expected to see, what they believed would happen.

AS YOU THINK...

We have many words that we think describe us and our behavior. We have attitudes about issues; in fact they are our thoughts about the issues. We are passionate about our teaching; in fact our thoughts create the passion. Our thoughts are manifest in our habits, in our desires, and in everything we do. Our relationships with our family and others are our thoughts about them, and our responses are our thoughts. As we "view" our past, it is nothing but thoughts. Jesus said, "As you think, so shall you be." And one of the great teachers of all times was neither the first nor the last to understand that concept.

Ralph Waldo Emerson suggested, "We become what we think about all day long." Lincoln admonished us with his well-known statement: "People are about as happy as they make themselves." We can all cite expressions that speak to this fact. The idea of anything is really the thought of that. Norman Vincent Peale told us to change our thoughts to change our world.

So many philosophers, teachers, thinkers in all disciplines have informed us about the fact that we are what we think. Everything originates in our thoughts. But as educators we seem to be too busy "thinking about the discipline of math or English" to remember that what we think about ourselves and about the learners in our charge will determine what happens more than the content we try to teach.

First, we bring ourselves. If we come angry or frustrated, the vibrations of our thoughts will transmit anger and frustration. If we believe this class is a "slow" class or individuals are "slow," those thoughts will be transmitted out; we will get back what we send out. Blaming the results on conditions outside of ourselves may make us feel exonerated, but it won't be the truth.

When we have a passion for our teaching, our thoughts create the behavior that transmits that passion. We are excited; we love the content and the context; we have fun and we believe that the students will learn. Should we feel the passion, yet in the back of our thoughts harbor the belief that the students just won't feel the same passion; the chances are that the students won't feel the same passion. That's the transmission. Passion is contagious unless we immunize against it by believing that it belongs to us alone.

Fortunately for us, we can change what happens in our classrooms because the future of what happens is in our thoughts. Work with teachers often centers on changing behaviors. It is energy wasted. Work must center on changing thoughts if we hope to have any change in behavior. We can teach methods and materials and curriculum "until the cows come home" without experiencing any change in behavior.

Until a person is willing to recognize that thoughts are the friends and the enemies and until a person is willing to acknowledge that it is the thought that needs changing, nothing will change. What happens reveals who you are. Your thinking determines your actions and your reactions. Whatever you think about, whatever your focus is, creates more of what you are thinking about whether you want it or not. If you focus on the "bad class," you will get more "bad class."

Your focus must change; your thoughts must change. If you expect change to occur anywhere else, you are going to be disappointed. You will feel you were right, the class is bad. Your thoughts were confirmed. Right! That is what you were thinking and where your focus was. Nothing else could happen—until you change your thoughts.

The importance lies in recognizing when thoughts are negative; that is where the change must occur. You will know by the way you feel whether the thought is helpful or harmful. You will know if the thought makes you feel good, it is positive; if it makes you feel uncomfortable and uneasy or even bad, you know that the thought is negative.

Change the thought immediately to a positive one. If you can't change to a positive thought on that particular subject, go to your positive thought reservoir and think about a positive thought from there. It is important to keep that reservoir filled; you never know when you need to lower the bucket into that supply. Always have those wonderful places and ideas to go to that make you happy and filled with love. You never know when you might need one.

As one of my students once said, "Why be miserable when you can be happy."

If I were teaching now, I would take a few minutes to monitor my thoughts. I would relax and just let them happen, as free a flow as possible. I would do this at the end of a day, a week, or when I had questions about what was happening. They might be about the past, present, or future; in each case I would focus on the thought/ energy. I would remember that I am creating my experience from these thoughts. The Law of Attraction is always at work. When I finished, I would assess whether or not they were positive or negative. I would test what I was feeling in each case. When I read a positive thought, what am I feeling? When I write or read a negative thought, what are my feelings? From this exercise, I could draw some conclusions about my thinking. This would help me with understanding what was going on in my classroom and in all areas of my personal and professional life.

I would have some actual data to work on changing my negative thoughts. It is our choice. Only we can make the shift; no one can do it for us.

Einstein said it well. We cannot solve the problems that we have with the same thinking that caused the problems. It is that thinking, that energy, that belief that we will see.

BELIEVEING IS SEEING!!

CHAPTER 5

JUST SUPPOSE

Suppose that we believed that whatever is in our experience we have attracted through the powerful Law of Attraction. Suppose we believed that this Law was responding to our thoughts. Suppose we understood that our thoughts send vibrations out that are responded to by powerful, scientific laws in the Universe. Suppose that we believed that what we give thought to is what we are inviting into our experience. Suppose we believed that as the thinker of the thoughts we can change what's happening by changing our thoughts. Suppose we believed that by changing a bad thought to a good one that we could change what comes to us.

JUST SUPPOSE

I knew that I could change the environment of my classroom by talking with my students about what kind of a classroom we wanted. At the beginning of my high school classes I would take the time to model the various kinds of teacher that I could be. I would ask them what their behavior would be in response to my behavior.

WHAT KIND?

"Suppose that I am a policeperson kind of teacher. I am here to keep order. I will tell you what to do and when to do it. I expect discipline. I expect you to behave. I will parcel out the assignments and I expect prompt responses. Expect me to discourage you if you talk too much. Don 't worry. I will answer your questions with finality.

How will you respond? How will you act?" Then I listened for their responses.

Their answers were right on target with what I had witnessed in rooms where the teacher acted like a cop: intense competition, which at its highest level leads to dishonesty; a lack of acceptance of all members; buck passing; avoidance of responsibility; unwillingness to cooperate; aggressive behavior toward group members and toward members outside the group; general irritability and unhappiness; a decrease in the level of work when the teacher is gone; complete chaos if a substitute teacher is in the room.

"Suppose that I am the laissez-faire teacher. I pretty much let you do what you want. I don't believe in rules; they just get broken. I haven't set any goals; maybe we can set some goals as we go along. Pretty much anything goes as long as you don't bother anyone else and, more importantly, don't bother me." I asked the students to tell me what their behavior would be.

Their answers again were predictable: disinterest; indifference; a lack of a purpose or goal; there would be no sense of achievement; if you don't care, how can we; at first we might think it was fun, but it wouldn't be because we wouldn't accomplish anything; it would be terribly boring; I don't want to spend my time doing nothing; I won't learn anything; I won't be ready for the next step; we wouldn't have anybody we could depend on; it would be horrible to spend all that time, 50 minutes a day, doing nothing; I wouldn't respect you: our class would be in chaos; we would be wasting our time.

"Suppose that I am a 'we-must-get-results' teacher. I know what's best for you and I know how to get it done. We have 400 pages in this book, and I've figured out how much we have to do every week to get through the book. We also will have a test every Friday to make sure that you have learned the material for the week. And we will stay on schedule. We have to make certain that we get through the book, because we have state tests in early June. You won't have to make many decisions; just follow along, pay attention, and you will be fine.

"Come to class prepared; we won't have much time to spend on any questions that you have. And you know I have nearly 200 kids in all of my classes, so I won't have much time for individual help. Any questions? Good! Then we understand each other. We should get along fine. I just expect results for my effort." As I modeled the behavior of a "we must get results" teacher, the discomfort grew with each statement. Again I asked what their response would be.

The responses were predictable: I don't respond well when I know my teacher doesn't have faith in me; I don't think you're going to get much work out of us; I can't imagine not getting help when I need it; I feel like you don't care about who we are; I feel like I can't talk to you and I better not admit it if I don't understand something; I'm not good at just rubber-stamping ideas; I really need to have something to say about what my class is like; it doesn't feel good; I can't imagine not being able to deviate from the lesson if something really interesting happens or somebody wants to share; you apparently are going to have your planned set of questions and answers, and we better not deviate.

JUST SUPPOSE—WHAT THEN?

The next question is the crucial one. It is where the Law of Attraction lies. "Obviously, we want a different kind of atmosphere in our classroom. What then do we want our class to be?"

I would outline what the course of study could be. They would have input; they could add. We would come as close as possible to shared goals for the class. When the course of study was agreed upon, I would present it to them by units. They were to record for me the level of interest (1 to 10 with 10 high) in each area. We would be aware that there would be varying levels of interest in the various areas. Knowing this, we would be respectful and participate whether or not it was an area of highest interest to us; this was very important because then we would have the same expectation for our areas of high interest. It was, in fact, the Golden Rule at work.

We did not have to agree with someone nor did all have to agree with us, but we would listen to the ideas of others and they to ours, and we would not be disrespectful or ever make fun of someone's idea or way of presenting it; all members would feel safe; we would know who's having trouble because our student network would keep us informed; we would be kind and supportive of each other's ideas and feelings; we would come in smiling and expecting good things to happen and we would leave knowing we had accomplished just that. We want our class to be a place that we want to come to because we will find wonder, astonishment, joy, appreciation, humor, goodwill and kindness.

It worked! No matter what the behavior of the students in other classes, once we had gone through the above exercise, their behavior in my class was great. Only rarely, would there be a detour in behavior; all it took was a pause in the day's activities and a reminder of what our agreement was. Usually all it took was, "Let's stop a minute and..." That would be as far as I could get. The response was, "We remember." And the behavior changed. I realize now that what we were doing with just that reminder was changing the thoughts of those who for that day had come with thoughts that had strayed, deviated, and for the moment were inviting into our room "things we did not want."

When we did the exercise, we had not just my thoughts and their vibrations being sent out into the Universe, we had all the members of the class agreeing and sending comparable thoughts and vibrations. The Law of Attraction becomes stronger as like thoughts merge. As we talked about what we wanted, like thoughts merged. No wonder it worked as if by magic. I say magic, because I often had other teachers or the principal walk by my room or visit my room and they were astounded because the "bad kids" were behaving, participating, respecting, smiling and not causing trouble. It was the Law of Attraction at work. It was the Deliberate Creation at work. It was the receiving of our desires at work.

Our room seemed like a magical box, though we all had placed in the box our desires, our thoughts about what we wanted our classroom to be. The thoughts were positive. We had created positive energy. Even if it were not in other places they visited, when they returned to their creation, they immediately were able to be in the positive energy. They were quite able to be positive even if the class before was negative. In the presence of the positive energy in our magic room, their resistance was not present. Their expressions of gratitude for what happened there and the feelings they had only brought more of the same. It truly was amazing.

I KNEW IT WORKED. But I did not know what to call it then. Now I know and now you know! It was the secret in the classroom. It was the universal Law of Attraction at work.

If I were teaching now, I would create my virtual classroom. I would visualize where it would be; what it would look like; what it would feel like, etc. I would say:

> "My classroom will be fun. I will...
> "My classroom will be bright. I will...
> "My classroom will be positive. I will...
> "My classroom will have high expectations. I will...
> "My classroom will be a beautiful place. I will..."

I would go there every day and spend a few minutes.

Create your virtual classroom. Remember, you are totally in charge of what you create. There's only one script and one camera filming; it is your script and your camera. As you go to your virtual classroom every day, journal what happens, how you feel. Notice how positive things and visits bring more of the same. Just suppose and watch what your thoughts can do.

CHAPTER 6

NO BETTER EXAMPLE

As teachers we need to understand fully that the Law of Attraction works whether or not we know about it. It has been working all the time and will continue to work in our classroom and in our lives. Because we spend so much of our lives as teachers with young people, we must become aware of what we are attracting into our environment. We literally think that environment into existence. That's powerful! We influence far beyond what we could possibly imagine.

Because you are thinking, the Law of Attraction is working. It is working whether you're speaking, listening, or reading. When you are thinking about the past, the present or the future, it is working. When you are introducing something, assigning a lesson, or watching the learners work, it is working. When you're correcting papers, or reading creative writing, it is working. When you're talking in the teachers room, talking to the counselor, reporting some happening to the principal, or talking to a parent, it is working. It does not stop working because you don't know about it or because you don't understand it or don't believe it. Because you are thinking, you are creating. Something will come from those thoughts.

Yes, you are creating your future life, but you are also transmitting vibrations that influence the lives of those students and persons around you who are receiving those vibrations. You are in charge of transmission. The teacher is the transmission tower, the issuer of the main vibrations in the classroom. In the eyes of the students, that's where the messages are coming from. The vibrations sent from the teacher are energy fields set up in the classroom. The thoughts of the teacher set up the messages transmitted.

Thoughts have frequencies; they can be measured. If the teacher is thinking negative things, negative vibrations are sent out and will find any negative vibrations that match. Thoughts are magnetic; they attract like thoughts. There is no better example of a transmission tower than a teacher in a classroom. The message received can only be that which is sent. You cannot watch a basketball game if you're tuned to a music channel any more than you can receive negative thoughts if positive thoughts are being sent.. What is transmitted is what you get. What the teacher transmits is what the students receive whether or not the teacher understands the principle or whether or not the teacher thinks something else is being transmitted.

CHANGING SIGNALS

But how do I change signals if the signal I'm sending is producing results that I do not want? The amazing thing is that you have a very easy way to know whether or not the vibrations you're sending are positive. You know by how you feel. If you feel good, send. If you don't feel good, you know immediately that is a negative transmission and not one that will produce positive results. How easy is that? Amazing and fascinating. Our feelings are our infallible guides. We need nothing else.

You can tell immediately what your tower is sending. If you feel good, you know that you are sending vibrations that are in harmony with what you want. If you have negative feelings, you know that you are sending vibrations that will bring you what you do not want.

I learned this first as a Bible verse: "Whatever you sow, you reap." For many years as I supervised student teachers in classrooms, the query so often was, "I don't understand why the students are reacting as they are." We would sit together and discuss what had happened. The student teacher would explain that the students made the day horrible, and it was horrible enough coming to school tired and angry. The students just didn't seem to respond to anything tried. But that was not really the situation. They did respond to what the teacher brought and they responded accurately.

The teacher came angry. The Universe does not try to change what you send. It is very accurate in its transmission. Whatever thoughts are present in the teacher's mind are those transmitted. Angry thoughts will find more angry thoughts. Like will attract like. Soon there are angry vibrations all over the place. There is no room for anything else. And there won't be until the teacher changes thoughts to positive, loving thoughts or at least thoughts that are not angry. The transmission tower has to send different signals to have different signals received. The thoughts of the teacher are primary.

Sometimes teachers tell me they feel insignificant. They feel powerless to change the atmosphere in the classroom. To the contrary; only they have the power to change it. The teacher, like any transmission tower, must have power to transmit. The power for teachers lies in their passion and commitment, their courage and confidence, and their ability and energy. Teachers who are unsure and who lack self-confidence will transmit those feelings. They are creating their world around them all the time. Their thoughts are shaping everything around them constantly. They must know who they are personally and professionally. "Know thyself" is the admonition and the power.

Because they do not know about or do not understand the Law of Attraction does not alter the scientific fact that it is always present and working. I don't understand much about the engine in my car; nevertheless, when I turn the ignition key on, I expect it to work for me. So it is with the Law of Attraction. Even if I don't understand it, it will still work. Even if I don't think about it, know about it or even believe it, it is still working.

I have listened to teachers in the teachers lounge. "Wow, Tim was really terrible today. I don't know what the problem was. He was fidgeting and talking; he just wouldn't settle down. I had to tell him so many times to be quiet; I was nervous and tired enough without him adding to it." When thoughts of nervousness and fatigue are being sent out, the transmission will be true; it cannot be anything else. The Law of Attraction will find other thoughts that match and bring them into your life.

Then I have watched teachers who heard about Tim. Tim's behavior was dependent largely on the thoughts from the transmission tower, the teacher. Negative thoughts from the next teacher would produce the same kind of behavior. Positive thoughts from another teacher would produce completely different behavior. I know from my own experience that I had so many students in my classes who behaved differently in my class than in other classes. I had students who were great learners in my class and who were wearing paths to the office or the dean's office from other classes.

Another statement coming from transmission towers that always intrigued was: "My students just act like they don't want to be here. They're absolute blobs in my class. But then, I don't know if I blame them; I don't really want to be here either. I'd rather be..."

Tower to students! I don't really want to be here. The transmission is always true; your thoughts will vibrate out with the utmost truth. Like the magnet they are, they will draw like thoughts back. The Law of Attraction says that when you think a thought you will attract like thoughts. "I don't want to be here" thoughts attract "I don't want to be here" thoughts. It cannot be otherwise.

When you walk into a classroom and you see students working together, being kind to each other, and you see the teacher interacting with a smile and a joyous demeanor, you see the happiness and joy of all in the room. You walk into another classroom and you see kids sniping at each other, refusing to cooperate with anyone, saying things that are sure to cause trouble, you generally find an atmosphere where there is a lack of respect for each other. It is a place where you see little learning, and much animosity. One is a place of excitement and joy; the other is a place of disrespect, rancor, and discontent.

As I look back on these scenarios, I realize that the Law of Attraction was at work. I didn't know what to call it because I didn't have a name for the secret. But memory tells me that the transmission towers were sending out thoughts, vibrations that matched what was coming from the students. I worked with the teachers to effect changes in behavior that would create changes in the atmosphere. How much easier it would have been for me if I had been able to explain the Law of Attraction. I knew it in my heart, but I didn't know how to explain to the teachers without seeming cruel that they were getting back exactly what they sent out.

MAKERS AND BREAKERS

Classrooms can be makers of dreams and aspirations and or they can be breakers of dreams and aspirations. Some of my saddest experiences in education have been those where I have seen dreams dashed, aspirations crumpled, and creativity squashed.

Places that don't allow students to grow are terrible gardens. Kids come to kindergarten full of zest and plenty of courage to try new things and be who they are. They even dare to say how they learn. Soon, however, they often find that their ideas are not valued, there are certain answers expected, and there are serious consequences for disagreeing with the teacher. The vibrations from the transmission tower are very clear. This is school. The eagerness and willingness to create are gone.

Affirmative thoughts are many times more powerful than negative thoughts. The affirmative thoughts of the students hang on as long as they can, but ultimately if there are negative thoughts transmitted to them, the negative will win. Fortunately for some, there are breathers from negative thoughts; students encounter a positive person and experience a reprieve.

In my graduate classes I have told teachers that when they really teach, they touch the souls of their students. I have come to believe that it is more than that. A teacher comes with thoughts; every minute those thoughts are sent out and the most powerful law in the universe goes to work. The vibrations reach the learners. Fortunately, sometimes the vibrations aren't strong enough to find like vibrations. But send out negative vibrations enough, and they will find like thoughts.

Remember the amount of time that these transmission towers—teachers—have with our children or learners at any level. Day after day for months. Month after month for years. It is important that we understand the magnitude of what our students experience. It is imperative that teachers have the knowledge, that they understand, and that they are able to know when they must change their thoughts to change their behavior.

You might want to try a little experiment. Pick a student who is causing you some difficulties. Write down as many statements as you can about the student. Allow room between each statement for a second statement or even a third. After you finish the first set, write a second statement that is better, more positive than the first and the second and so on. Indicate whether you feel better about the second. Remember, your barometer is the way that you feel. You also can write one statement that describes a problem, followed by a series of statements that you can test.

Document what happens around you as you become more adept at monitoring your feelings and change your behavior accordingly

The teacher sends out thoughts; the vibrations reach the learner. The transmission tower sends and the receiver picks up the transmission. No better example can be found.

CHAPTER 7

TEACHING IN THE UNIVERSE OF THINKING

The tool of our profession is thought. The universe of thinking is our workplace. It is the universe in which we do our teaching and learning. Consider thought as something we create at all times, and something that is created around us by others at all times. This creative process is our connection to the divine and the infinite.

Quantum physics has given us information about consciousness, energy, thought, and other universal laws of nature that govern all of our lives, yet many view the information with skepticism. Many prefer to think that their lives are governed by circumstances, by some predetermined destiny over which they have little or no control.

Physicists have known for some time that what we once thought was solid matter is actually vibrating energy, a universe of unlimited potential. This is a source that has no bounds and is always available to fill our orders. But it cannot fill what is not ordered, nor can it deliver properly when the address is not correct or the order is not specific. The energy source never ceases. We can harness it for our personal and professional use.

We accept the wonders of science that affect us; we understand the liberating influence much of science has had on our lives. Technology, travel, health, energy, space or any of the many discoveries decade by decade, year by year, moment by moment engage our fancy. We accept most of the advances and learn to live with them, appreciate, and come to think of them as a normal part of our existence.

That is, until we enter the realm of the mind, the domain of thought, the energy of consciousness that we cannot see. These are the areas that should concern us the most. As persons and educators we need to understand the advances made in understanding consciousness, energy, thought, learning, the brain, knowing and being. We have grown up with a psychological paradigm that is difficult to change.

We have been taught that we are born with certain capacities, and that we are born with a brain that is limited to the neurons that are present at birth. The disaster is that we are told that we will lose neurons each day and hour that we live, neurons never to be repaired, changed, or replaced. Is it any wonder that we grow mindless as we "lose our neurons"?

It is difficult for us to accept the findings of quantum physics, neuroscience, and cell biology, and certainly more difficult to accept changes to our psychological paradigm. Understandings about neuroplasticity will change that paradigm if we allow the science to inform our knowing.

THE SCIENCE OF NEUROPLASTICITY

The science of neuroplasticity, the ability of the brain to form new connections, changes everything. Because the brain has the capacity to form new connections, it has the potential to compensate for changes in the environment in case of injury or trauma. Genes are not in control of our behavior. We have choices; for that we have responsibility. Since the concept of neuroplasticity holds keys to changing how we view the brain, we must know what is known. The lives of our children, those in our charge, are the recipient of our knowledge or our lack of knowledge.

The great news for us as teachers is that we are all born with a far more plastic, adaptable, changeable brain than we have been taught and believed. It is not the closed system we thought it to be. An open system allows for adaptation and change. The idea of one location, one function in the brain, the idea that complete localization is present in the brain is an idea that has been hard to change. When we change our thinking to an idea of plasticity, we open ourselves up to tremendous opportunities for our teaching and learning.

When we know that we need to exercise the brain to keep it fit just as we exercise our bodies to keep them fit, we must view our tasks differently. Our bodies do not work as well when they do not have the benefit of workouts. So it is with our brains. The fewer intentional workouts our brains get, the less fit they are. The brain needs to be stimulated.

The research done indicates that this intentional practice can help the brain recover from age-related losses. Imagine what intentional practice can do to help young minds recover from losses suffered from a lack of stimulus, inaction, and boredom. We need to think to have our brains function well. It is preferable to think about new things, learn about new things that will cause the brain to function at higher levels. Novelty requires more focus and attention than that required for repetitive activity.

SYNCHRONICITY

With this awareness we can dismiss "coincidence" and believe in the divine intelligence operating in our universe. Of course, once you believe it, you will truly see it working every day. Synchronicity is not a passive speculative principle. It is here; it works, and you are a part of it. Believe it or not. See it or not.

Thoughts are energy that resonates in the universe vibrating at enormous speed. Once you accept that thought can possibly exist outside of you, you are on your way to understanding synchronicity.

We are all aware of anecdotes from our own experience or that of others where thoughts have influenced other thoughts at great distances. Physicist John S. Bell's theorem of nonlocality in quantum physics demonstrates how particles affect the actions of other particles that are far apart. Edward Lorenz's butterfly effect tells us that something happening in Costa Rica can have great influence on happenings in San Diego or Seattle or Boston.

Certainly scientists have proven over and over again that all things are connected. I am reminded of the great thought from Chief Seattle: "This we know, all things are connected like the blood that unites us all. Man did not weave the web of life; he is merely a strand in it. Whatever he does to the web, he does to himself." How can it be less true at the level of personal experience? When we understand this interconnectedness, we must surely know the importance of living in harmony with the vibrations that swirl around us.

When we are in harmony we find ourselves in the world of infinite possibilities, as has been described by so many scientists and philosophers. The quantum field of the physicists is the field of unlimited potential for us in our personal and professional lives. Pure potentiality, infinite possibilities, unlimited potential—all are ways of describing the Universe of consciousness that contains everything that we could possibly desire. When our thoughts and feelings are in harmony with our actions, we realize these infinite possibilities. The Source, the Universe, God has provided this field of pure possibility for us. The sky is the limit. Things happen that are magical. But it is not magic. When we live our lives in tune with what we are feeling and thinking, the roads we take and the paths we travel are much smoother

Alignment starts with self. All solutions start with self. Ralph Waldo Emerson said, "What lies behind us and what lies before us are small matters compared to what lies within us." Being responsible for our thoughts and behavior is necessary. We must understand that we are totally responsible for the quality of our experiences. We are totally responsible for our thoughts and our emotions.

We cannot be in harmony when we are having bad thoughts about ourselves, when we are feeling helpless, unworthy, and unattractive. When we are self-deprecating, we cannot feel love for ourselves. And when we do not feel love for ourselves, we cannot feel it for anyone else. This makes it impossible to be in harmony with the Source, consciousness. When we cannot be accepting of ourselves, we cannot be accepting of anyone else.

Whatever you project, you can be certain that like vibrations will be returned to you. From self, the vibrations extend to others. How we feel about ourselves vibrates out to others and connects to the vibrations of the Universe. We get like vibrations back. When we realize that we are the source of all things that return to us in like kind, we know that our life, our future, is our responsibility.

When we make the choice to accept others, to love, we gain power because we are in harmony with the Universe, our connections are positive. When we reject or hate others, we are out of harmony and can be certain that we will receive the same things back. We have lost power and control. When we become angry at someone, that person has power over us. Only we can solve that problem.

As we understand our connectedness with others, we are achieving the harmony that we long for. We achieve the peace that we desire. We find the compassion in others that we send out. We feel the love from others that we have extended to them. We can be certain that the Universe provides "in-kind" contributions. We are the thinker of our thoughts and only we can change them or retain them to have the kind of life we desire.

When we are in harmony and we connect with others in harmony with the laws of the Universe, we experience the interconnectedness that provides us with the "magic" of synchronicity. We now receive the blessings of the "pure potentiality" of the Universe.

Imagine your classroom as an arena of pure potentiality. Imagine that the universe of your classroom has everything in it that you need to have the environment that you want and deserve. Imagine that you are in charge of that universe. Imagine that you hold the key to that pure potentiality. Imagine that you are the architect, the designer of this universe. You now have at your disposal all that you imagined. In the Universe, no distinction is made between your perception of reality and reality.

In my early days of studying the brain, consciousness and perception were the realm of psychologists and philosophers. Physicists were scientists who were definitely not interested in these areas considered apart from pure science. In the mid 1970s, when Fritjof Capra, a physicist, was invited to join us at Oregon State University to present seminars for our teachers, particularly our science teachers and professors from around the state, the subject was neuroscience and learning. It was clear in my personal conversation with Capra and in his presentations that physicists no longer were at arm's length from Eastern mysticism, consciousness, and heretofore "nonscientific topics."

USING THE SAME NEURONS

When we work with learners it is useful to know that they will use the same neurons if they are actually looking at an object or if they only remember it. There is much research that shows us that the same neurons fire whether we are actually seeing an object or happening or whether we are remembering it.

Scientists all over the world now are studying and researching the physics of consciousness, reality and perception, memory and more. In physics, scientists have proved that reality isn't separate from the observation of it. We need to apply what we have learned to our classroom of pure possibility. We want to create a classroom environment where we use that potential of every learner.

If we have a negative perception of a room and group, we need to change it. We do not need to be stuck in that perception of reality, our reality at that moment. We need to activate the potential in the room; we need to release the potential of the consciousness available. We need to change our perception to a positive perception. We can change the environment by changing our perception of it. We don't have to see our class in the same way.

If I were teaching now, I would imagine my classroom or any learning environment as one that contained all that I needed. I would visualize it all. Every student/learner is capable. All have possibilities for success. I would look at each student and expect success. I would look again and I would see success happening. I would only have thoughts about the enormous potential present. Now as I stay focused on this imaginary arena, my perception is different. Now I am free to imagine what I desire.

Remember, your brain doesn't distinguish between what you imagine and what is real. Now you imagine the success that you want; now you imagine every single detail of what you want this learning environment to be. Now you send out vibrations to each student of what your expectations are. You send your messages with love, acceptance, and enthusiasm.

Your images of your successful learning environment will be the tap to the Universal consciousness. Your dream classroom as you imagined will be manifested if your images are clear, your thoughts are positive and clear, and your thoughts and behavior are aligned and in harmony. You will feel and experience the interconnectedness of all things.

CONSIDER THE IMPLICATIONS

Consider the implications for our professional and personal lives.

Most of us are painting on such small canvases. We believe that we understand our reality. After all, we have been told so many times "to get real" when we have walked to the edge of our canvas and have taken a peek around. Perhaps we even set up our easel and painted a new picture. We were told so often to stay within the lines. Sad, when our ability to imagine and paint new pictures is the tool for creating our new realities.

The more we can imagine success and feel successful in what we desire, the more we can perceive that success. Those images create reality for us if the images are clear. We are tuned in to the Universe of pure potentiality that can deliver our dreams. The minute that we doubt, or fear failure, or believe that we don't deserve what we are asking for, we cloud the messages; the thoughts/vibrations are not pure and clear, and we have confused our order to the Universe.

When we go to the library we ask for a specific book or have a specific question. If we don't know what we want and tell the librarian that we are not certain and we tell her to just bring us any book, she would not be able to fill our order. We would not send an order to a mail-order house and order just anything. They would not be able to fill our order. So it is with the Universe; it can only fill the orders that we send. And it will do that whether it is something that we want or don't want. So it is with our students. When we send out mixed messages, their universe cannot fill our orders; they will be jumbled and we will be angry because they didn't do as we asked. We must be certain that the transmission is exactly the message that makes our wishes clear. We have placed an "order" for exactly what we want to happen.

Our images, our orders, our desires must be clearly delineated. We must be committed to our images; they will become the reality in our lives. We need to make certain that the images that we have are those that we really want. Those images of what we want our classroom to be must be clear. As we imagine, our thoughts will connect with like thoughts. As you continue to make your images clear and you vividly repaint your canvas just the way that you want it, it must appear that way.

You must make certain that there are no extraneous pictures left or projected, that the images are such that you already feel that they exist. Check it out and experience it; enlarge it and touch it in your mind. Let go of any thoughts that dim or cloud your clear images; don't let fear enter the picture of your mind,

Expect it to happen just as you see it. This is necessary for your "order" to be filled.

You must expect your order to be filled just as you have placed it. If any thought of "it probably won't happen," "these kids won't understand," "I don't deserve these great things," or "why hasn't it happened already," you have clouded your expectation attitude. If you have created a classroom that is "beyond anything that you can comprehend" you will not expect delivery. Your order will be lost because of lack of a clear address. You must check your order to make certain that you have not ordered great things that you don't really expect. You must have expectations that are unlimited to fit your unlimited desires. When your desires, your images, and your expectations are not the same, your expectations will not be realized.

Choose a perception of a successful classroom; visualize all that perception entails; expect the very best to happen. Check the feelings that you have as you monitor the process. Your feelings will tell you if any of your thoughts are contradictory to your desires. The thoughts will not feel good. Walk through the room several times to make certain that you have pictured/imagined exactly what you desire. If a negative action, statement, or happening occurs, return to the positive visualization of what you want/expect. Always return to the positive (the opposite picture of the negative); see and feel the change. Record what happens.

CHAPTER 8

KNOWING AND ASKING FOR WHAT YOU WANT

An environment exists in every classroom—a positive environment of success and joy, or one of little hope, boredom, and despair. The power of intention is infinitely powerful. Of great importance is creating an environment by intention, rather than by default. Our beliefs and attitudes and understanding make a difference. Just letting it happen is not good enough. We will see in our environment what we believe about our learners.

Over the many years in education, I have asked these questions many times. Do you know what you want to learn? Do you know what you want your classroom to be like? Do you know what you want your life to be? What is your vision for your school? What do you want your first day of school to be? What do you want the behavior of your students to be? What do you want your relationship with parents to be like? There are many more questions you could add to the list. But right now ask yourself, "Do I know what I want today to be like?"

As you ponder your answer, I would like to suggest some ideas about the answers that I received. So often there were long pauses before any answer was suggested. For the most part, the answers started with what they didn't want. While there is some value that can be gained from knowing what you don't want, it really only works to your advantage if you recognize that information as a guidance system that immediately points you toward what you do want.

WHY DO I GET WHAT I DON'T WANT?

It is of the utmost importance to understand that what you don't want becomes what you get unless you change your thoughts. When your thoughts are about what you don't want, you attract like thoughts and those thoughts attract more like thoughts and you have a picture that looks much like a string of pearls, one thought attached to another and another and on and on. The Universe doesn't distinguish between the thoughts about what you want or don't want. It only gives you what you think about. Your thoughts are the creator of your NOW.

"I don't want my classroom to be noisy." "I don't want my classroom to be a sad place." "I don't want, I don't want, I don't want."

But my question is, "Do you know what you want?"

"Well, I know I don't want it to be like my English class was." And the conversations continue. "My math teacher never explained things; I don't want my class to be like that." "My science teacher could never answer hard questions." "My second grade teacher was mean to some kids." "My seventh grade teacher made fun of some kids." "My P.E. teacher made jokes about kids who couldn't do some of the exercises or run a mile." "My social studies teachers never allowed opinions to be discussed if he disagreed with them."

Only if those thoughts are replaced with the opposite thoughts, thoughts that turn into positive thoughts that express what you do want, are they of any benefit. Only when you recognize the importance of knowing what place your thoughts have in bringing to you exactly what you are thinking about can you control what comes into your life. So it is with your classroom or for that matter any other of your relationships. Understand that the Law of Attraction works whether or not you believe that it exists.

Do you know what you want?

Take a few minutes to answer the question. What is it that I really want in my classroom, in my life, in my relationships, etc.? Make separate columns if necessary. When you finish, it might be helpful to prioritize your list.

You must clearly understand the answer to that question. That is what you must focus on. That is what must have your attention. Whatever you give your attention to is what will be manifest in your life. Remember, if you continue to think about what you don't want, that is what will be reflected in your experiences.

THE WORRY TREE

Sometimes student teachers would start our conversations with "worry" statements. "I'm really worried about keeping order." "I'm really worried about not knowing the material well enough." "I'm worried about how much energy I will need." "I'm worried that the kids won't like me." "I'm worried about the salary I'm making; I don't know if I can make ends meet."

The worry tree is full of ornaments, each a shiny beacon to what the future holds. Worry creates an imaginary set of "I don't wants." There is an expression I've heard many times: "Worry is like a rocking chair; it gives you something to do, but it doesn't get you anywhere." Unfortunately, worry gets you the imaginary things that you don't want; that's where your thoughts are. "Worry is the interest paid by those who borrow trouble" fits better with the Law of Attraction. Worry is just another way to bring into your life what you don't want.

Once you understand that you create your experiences and that there are no accidental happenings that occur, you can start to create your dreams and desires. Once you believe that nothing can come into your experience without you inviting it there, you will have passed the midterm examination—you understand that what you ask for you get. Only when you task yourself with monitoring your thoughts, will you be able to change the situation. The classroom is no different. What you have manifested in your classroom is what you ask for through your thoughts. Only when you acknowledge that you have "invited" whatever is happening to you into your experience, will it be possible to change it.

If you don't believe that, ask the students which of their classes are different, which classes have the qualities that you want in yours. Go visit. See what happens. Observe what the teacher says and does. Be aware of your own feelings as you look at students from your class who are totally different in the class that you are observing. Write down specific statements of the teacher; watch the response of the students. Ask the teacher what he/she was feeling at the time. Ask the teacher for specific thoughts. It is guaranteed that positive thoughts have made the difference.

As I have worked in education over the years, I have heard much of what we don't want. And we seem to be getting many of those unwanted things. Fortunately for me, I have also had teachers who were totally positive. They practiced The Law of Attraction although they never named it for me. I came to know the power of positive thought early.

MY MISS WHITE

Miss White, a true mentor, was a wizard at teaching with only positive statements. When we were taking any of our physical education theory classes with her, she would say, "You always tell a student what you want them to do; never tell them what you don't want them to do." It was present in everything that we did with her and what she did with us.

In swimming classes, we were always to say what we wanted the swimmer to do. We would sometimes forget and tell a student, "Don't kick that way." Her response was swift and consistent, "Only the positive. Tell them how you want them to kick."

In stunts and tumbling classes, we were required to make cards for each stunt or tumbling routine that said exactly what we wanted them to do. She was particularly strict in those classes; she said it prevented accidents.

It seems so obvious to me now. She was a master at the Law of Attraction. She was a master in the same class with the great artists and musicians who have lived across the centuries. She was teaching us the *secret:* Ask, Believe, and Receive.

There are so many signposts and signals along the way if we look and listen. My mother's way of saying it was, "Honey, you can catch more flies with sugar than with vinegar." "If you don't like the crop that you are reaping, you need to change the seed you are sowing." "Keep your mind off the thing you don't want by keeping your mind on the things you do want." We have heard and read many more. We know and feel but often do not practice these with our thinking. When we do, our students will respond.

When we send positive, loving, caring thoughts out, that's the frequency they receive. When we send negative, hateful, callous thoughts out, that's the frequency they get. The thoughts, the vibrations that are sent are the vibrations the magnets get. I have even seen students try hard to change the channel. They drop out; they fight back; they say positive things hoping to get some positive response back; they blame themselves and vow to change. But the channel changer is in the teacher's mind. That is where the thoughts must change.

Too many times I have heard the pleas and frustrated comments: "My students don't listen. I have told them so many times that I don't want them to talk in class." "I have told them not to bend their legs when they do that stroke." "How many times do I have to tell them not to forget to put their names on their papers." "I don't know how many times I have asked them not to use that language." Don't, don't, don't. How many times must I tell them not... I've seen the law in action, because when I watch the learners, the teacher gets exactly what's been sent out. And the discipline problems begin and never end.

When I visited the University Elementary School at UCLA with a group of my graduate students when Madeline Hunter was the leader there, it was clear that positive thoughts were being sent out. I now know how well the Law of Attraction was operating in positive ways. I never once heard any teacher or any other person working with children tell them what not to do. I never heard bad language, but I did hear wonderful big, interesting, and fascinating words; I was told that any language that was inappropriate was replaced with words that were more interesting. Children came into the classroom and were immediately engaged. Never did I hear a "Don't do..." Everything was what to do. There was nothing but positive expectations. It was an interesting and positive, successful learning environment

Do you know what you want? Can you state clearly in positive terms what you do want, not what you don't want?

When you tell your class that you are disappointed with their behavior, you are starting in the wrong place. You must start with yourself. You must believe that it starts with you, the transmitter of the thoughts. It can be no other way.

You must know yourself and why you are teaching, Ask yourself the question, "Why am I here?" When students ask you that question, what will your answer be? You must be able to say that you are where you want to be. If you cannot say that, your days will be difficult and perhaps you shouldn't be teaching.

If you lay the blame for what you don't have anywhere but where it lies, you will feel the same anger and frustration tomorrow as you feel today. You will experience many years in teaching, frustrating day after frustrating day. You will be one of those who finishes a career the way it started on the first day—"I don't know why I chose this punishment."

The problem with such a career is the punishment of the students. If you choose to inflict that punishment on yourself day after day, that is one thing. The unholy thing about it is the number of young lives that you might have injured or destroyed. Anyone who is angry every day in the classroom should not be there. Those who feel the thrill of power over young lives should not be there. For those who cannot feel joy and passion about such an important profession, there are jobs available with less disastrous influence. For those who blame young lives for their inadequacy, there are other areas of employment.

It would have been so much easier had I known earlier in my career of teaching teachers and other school personnel about the Law of Attraction. It is so much simpler than all of the many names we have dreamed up to try to accommodate, name, or otherwise try to change negative behavior of school people. Be positive, we say. But how much easier it would be to simply give them the *secret.* You can change the experiences you are living by changing your thoughts. That's where the transmission takes place, and you are in charge of that tower.

CHAPTER 9

GETTING THERE FROM HERE

During the years that I spent as a counselor, teacher, and administrator, I was asked the same question: "But how do I get to where I want to be from where I am? It seems like such a long distance." "But how do I become what I want to become? It seems like such an insurmountable task." "But how do I teach the way I want to? I just don't know where to start." The underlying question was the same: How do I get where I want to go from where I am? It is the age old dilemma. How do I get to the finish line?

You must start from where you are. Simply, you cannot start anywhere else because you are where you are. It seems like such a simple answer in context. Usually the comments would start. "But I don't like where I am." "I don't know how to take the next step." "I'm confused about where I want to go." "It seems so easy when I watch my friends." "I'm really trying to get started." "Everything seems to work against me." "I guess I just don't deserve it."

All of those comments instruct. They show resistance patterns that prevent us from "getting there."

You cannot run a race unless you know where the starting line and finish line are. You know the distance, what the record times are and you know the competitors. Would you just go to the starting line and start running? Would you expect to start in the middle of the race? You would start at the starting line.

Suppose you are preparing to take a trip. You decide your destination. You decide how you will travel there. You decide when you will start. You know you can only start from where you are when you begin the trip. Each day of the trip has its own beginning. Whether it's the first day, the second, or the last day, you can only start from where you are.

So it is with our personal destinations, the destinations to our desires, our dreams. We can only start from where we are at any given moment. We must release the thoughts that tell us we should be somewhere else. They are resistances that hold us back, just as the strong wind in a race is a resistant force.

So it is with our work in the classroom. We must know where we want to go, where we want to be, what we want to do. We must be clear about that vision, those goals. Then we must be clear about where we are. That's where we must start.

BEING HAPPY AT THE STARTING LINE

We must be happy to start where we are. If we are unhappy about where we are, we immediately are offering thoughts of resistance. If we think we should be someplace else, we are offering thoughts of resistance. Knowing that we do not want to be there can help us determine where we want to be, but wishing that we were somewhere else is the wishing wind of resistance.

The source of our energy supplies all we need to move, to change our classroom to what we want it to be. Thoughts that are in harmony with that source within us offer no resistance. We move freely toward our goal. When we ask, we receive, because everything is available to us. When we desire, our attention is focused. We have begun to create our reality. Remember, we will get what we are thinking about whether or not we want it.

Sometimes it is difficult to understand the concept of being happy about where we are as the start of our journey. But being happy with what we are and what we have allows us to move forward. A great place to start is by being grateful for what we have. We always have something for which we can be grateful. If we are unhappy about where we are and what we have, it is impossible to move forward with those negative thoughts. Those thoughts can only bring bad feelings; from those feelings we can determine the nature of our thoughts. We must think positive thoughts to move forward. Then we can think about what we want, where we want to be, where we want to go with eagerness and anticipation.

On one occasion when we were talking about this concept, a teacher told me that when he felt ill or was feeling grumpy, he would "trick" himself into feeling better by being nice to the first person he met at school. He said, "By being nice to the first person that I met, it changed the corner of my mouth and the tenor of my entire day."

We decide that we want our classroom to be different. We change when we say, "OK, this is where I am, and this is where I want to be. I want my classroom to be filled with joy and anticipation, with eagerness to learn, and with cooperation and compassion."

Now we have a starting line. We must be the first to enter this race. We must understand that we are the creator of this environment. We must come with joy and anticipation; we will know by the way that we feel whether or not we do. When the bell rings, check your feeling when the students enter. Do you have feelings of joy and anticipation? If you do, that's what you will transmit. If you don't, you must change your thoughts to something that brings joy and anticipation. What you are thinking will be transmitted to the students.

When the students enter, check your thoughts about learning. Do you have feelings of anticipation about what you will learn and teach this day, or are you having feelings of boredom? You will transmit what your thoughts are to the students. What you feel will tell you what your thoughts are. When the students enter, are you thinking about hassles with students yesterday, about difficulties with Joe and Jane, or about how uncooperative some of the students were? You will know that you are transmitting those negative thoughts by the way you feel.

The essence—to get from where you are to where you want to go—starts NOW with you. The route is yours to plan; you are the creator from beginning to end. Winston Churchill said, "You create your own universe as you go along."

Sometimes the responses indicate that teachers feel alone and not appreciated. "But, that's all great on paper." "Have you ever been with 35 middle school students?" "You know I have a life outside of school." "I don't think you realize what an intensive job teaching is. I have 30 plus kids six periods a day; I don't have time to think."

Yes. I have had 72 junior high kids in one class. As a matter of fact, it was the very first class that I ever taught. And yes, I know that we all have life outside of our professional choices. Teaching is intensive and challenging; that's why I loved it so much. For years I had 30 plus kids in six classes a day. You are not alone in these experiences.

WHEN WE MAKE THE CHOICES

Choosing to teach is conscious. When we make that choice, we know something about the school scene. It is something we have all lived for many years. It is not a job that we enter blindly. It is not a blank slate. As a matter of fact, it is the one profession that we all enter with well-constructed desires, beliefs, and expectations. We have constructs of what we want when we teach and I suspect more constructs of what we don't want. These constructs form a fairly well-defined starting line.

When we enter our classroom each day, each hour, we must monitor our thoughts. We can recognize negative thoughts when we have feelings that are bad. It is then that we need to change the thoughts. When we have good feeling we know that we are in tune with a positive way forward. When we start the day by telling the secretary in the office that we hope today will not be as bad as yesterday, we have set up the day to be like yesterday. When we tell our teaching neighbor we had a wonderful day yesterday, it was so much fun and such a joy to be here, we have set up our day to be fun and joyous. We know we are on the right track because we feel joy and cheerfulness. We know immediately by the way we feel.

We can transmit only what we are thinking. When the students enter our classroom, they are tuned to our channel. They can wish they were on another channel, but they have only our channel available. Our transmission must be accepting and approving, cheerful and joyous. The environment must be challenging and inventive. We must transmit attitudes of candor and courage. Our thoughts must be constructive and cooperative; inspired and humble. We need to be kind and charitable; spontaneous and serene. When we act in responsible, respectful, unselfish and caring ways, our environment will be nurturing and powerful. These are the signposts on the road we travel.

This may sound overwhelming. They are merely values and attitudes that are available to us in our lives. We merely choose the positive over the negative. When we think only positive thoughts about our journey, the destination, the environment in our classroom will be what we want. Our built in guidance system will tell us whether our transmitted thoughts are those that we must have to reach our desires.

If I were teaching now, I would keep a journal/notepad or just a calendar on my desk or in a handy place. Or perhaps I would ask a student to record. When a negative thought occurred, I would write it down; often it would take just one word to describe the incident or circumstance. At the end of the period or designated time, I would replace the negative word with a positive one. Or I would have a student observer text message or e-mail me with a positive word or statement. At the end of the period, I would discuss the process with the students, or I would demonstrate the technique the next day for the students to learn and discuss what happens when the negative is changed to positive.

Yes, we can get there from here. And what a journey it will be. And we will know by the way we feel when we are "there." Of course, there will always be another journey ahead.

CHAPTER 10

THE STARTING LINES

How many times and in how many ways have you encountered starting lines or beginnings?

So many times in my career, I have told students, counselees, friends, or my own children that you must start from where you are; it is the only starting line that you have. I expect that I have said words to that effect in so many different ways that it would be useful to illustrate the intuitive sense I had without knowing what to call it. I realize now that so many others have said it in many other ways.

Alcoholics Anonymous requires that you say and understand that you are an alcoholic; they require that you continue to know that you are an alcoholic who cannot take a drink. They know that once you change your thought from no drinking to taking a drink, you are on the skids. It is the simple process of changing a thought to take a drink to a thought not to take a drink. We make it enormously complex in our minds. At least, so it seems to me.

As I've talked with people with problems of this nature, they are always worried about the "What ifs?" "What if I go to a friend's house and I'm served a drink?" "What if I will embarrass somebody who is trying to be nice to me?" What if, what if, what if? When all these thoughts about alcohol are present, the chances are pretty high that sooner or later one of the "what ifs" will get you; that's the simple Law of Attraction. I believe that "what if" is the other side of fear. Just think what lies on the other side of fear—all those incredible things that "what if" kept you from doing, trying and being.

There is always a starting place for our thoughts. When designing masters and doctors degrees, I always have students start with what they "bring to the table." We set up a graphic of three columns. In the first column they give all the information about who they are, what they have experienced, and what educational experience they bring. The third is a clear picture of where they want to go, be, and do. The middle column is left for the route to get from column one to three.

It is sometimes very difficult to get students to accept where they are. The conversations are often filled with doubt and limitation. When the first column is difficult "to extract" from the student, I always know that there is a probable difficulty with the other two. I realize what I ask them to do is to believe in themselves; yes, to be where they are is OK.

Once they change their thinking to positive energy, the scene changes. They start to talk about all that they have done, what they have studied, what they have achieved, and the start of column three is underway. Once they accept and have gratitude for where they are, they have found their starting line for the next race. With that acceptance and gratitude in place, they can ask, and believe, and receive.

When students start designing research for papers, theses, and dissertations, there is an enormous block in their thinking. There is a cultural mystique about research. Most students don't believe they are capable of doing "research." They have a vision of research as something mysterious that happens to someone else, someone brighter and more talented. They have visions of statistical data and dreams of charts and tables that they don't or couldn't understand.

I tell the masters degree students in my research class that before they exit, they must be able to tell me that they feel competent to proceed to a doctoral degree if they choose. They give me all kinds of exclamatory remarks. "I don't want a doctoral degree." "I could never do that."

I assure them that it will happen. Thinking positively will give them courage to try things, to venture further, to be creative, to know that they are researchers every day in the classroom, and that they are capable of doing whatever they can think of. I realize now that I was asking them to believe that where they were was perfectly all right, and that I believed that they could do this task. To their amazement, on the last day of the class as they presented their work, every student was able to verbalize confidence to go on. They had changed their thinking.

It is the *secret*. Ask, believe, and receive with gratitude.

As I think about all the classes on discipline that I have taught, I realize that I was asking students to accept students where they were. There is nowhere to go if you don't start where they are. That does not mean accept the behavior they are exhibiting; it means recognize the goal of the behavior. It is the only starting place there is. It is the only place to ask for a change.

ABOUT DISCIPLINE

Unless you know what the goal of the behavior is, you will not know how to get the change. The goal manifests the thinking, which determines the behavior. I have found that there are three main goals.

The first is to get attention; the second is get control of the situation—power; the third is to get even, to get revenge. These three cover most of the situations that occur.

It is interesting to note that the three are incremental. If you deal with a problem as if it is an attention-getting behavior by giving them attention in some way that they don't expect and it doesn't solve the problem, the chances are great that you're dealing with power or revenge. If you deal with a situation as attention-getting or power and the problem is not solved, you probably have a learner who is trying to get even. A power struggle is deadly for a teacher; I have never seen a teacher win one. You must extricate yourself by backing out. Work to give them some control of their learning situation, often with simple choices, and you can win. I have experienced attempts at power struggles at all levels of my teaching, including at the university level in graduate classes.

When you get to the third main type, revenge, you must take a look at what you have been doing with the student that would cause him or her to want to "get back at you." If you don't know or can't figure it out, ask the student(s). In many cases a simple, "Let's start over; what we are doing isn't working for us," will solve the problem.

There is one additional behavior that some students will use; they will try to get you to believe that they can't do the work. They will usually sit back and do little or nothing to convince you that they are unable. It's a very passive kind of behavior. Unless you deal with the goal, where they are, you will not get the change in behavior that you desire.

My granddaughter and I were talking recently about the behavior of students in her classes last year that bothered her and others because it interfered with the learning process. She described what some kids were doing. I suggested what I would have done in those cases. She thought it would have worked and solved many problems.

She said, "Grandma, you have to put this in your book. It would make it so much better for kids."

One of the tenets usually put forth in discipline is consistency. Treat everyone exactly the same. This sounds great; the problem is that the same behavior in different students might have different goals and, therefore, must have different responses. Where each student is, must become the starting line. The outcomes desired are the same, but the roads to get there might be different.

Our options always remain open whether or not we are aware of them. Our ability to see the possibilities can be clouded by our beliefs, what we have been taught. The choices we make may seem like the only ones available because they are the only road map that we have. We have traveled those routes for so long that they have become our habits.

THOSE PESKY CHOICES AGAIN

Every day, with no exception, we make thousands of choices; we choose to do the same things. "It's always been that way." "I've always done it this way." "It's the way that I was taught." "It's the only way to go; I'm not comfortable doing it a different way." "It was good enough for them, it's good enough for me." "I'm afraid to try anything else; it seems OK to me." "It gets me through this boring task." We've all heard these and many more ways of explaining why we do things "our way."

What we really need to understand about these decisions we make thousands of times a day is that each time we make the decision, we are making a choice. We cannot expect a different result from the same choice. If we want a different result, something has to change. Make the same choice, get the same result. As I said in Chapter 4, Einstein said it well. "You can't expect to solve a problem using the same thinking that caused the problem."

It is these daily choices in our classrooms that create the environment that we have. If we want it to be different, we must make some different choices. If we want a different picture, we must change the canvas, the beliefs that we have. We must change the picture that we have, our perceptions of what we have and can have, and we must change our paintbrushes and paint, our thoughts. Then we must change the way that we paint, our behavior.

When you change your perception, your thoughts, and your behavior, you will have a different painting. When you decide that you want a different picture, a different classroom, you are the solution. You must make different choices. You cannot get a different classroom making the same choices that produced the environment that you don't want. Many of the choices we make are conscious and many are unconscious choices. What is paramount to know and understand is that the unconscious choices carry as much weight in the vibrational universe as the conscious ones. The unconscious choices that are made as habit, as old beliefs, as perceptions about self and others, are returned to us just as readily as the conscious ones.

The essence to changing the choices lies in accepting where you are at the time of choice. The essence lies in knowing where and what the starting line is. Remember, there is no other place to start. Change starts from where you are.

Today is the gift. Be grateful for the gift.

CHAPTER 11

HOW SOON? HOW LONG?

"How soon do you expect me to be able to do this? I can't change that fast." Or: "It will take me a little time to make that change; I can't do that overnight." If you want to change what's happening in your life and you want to change what you ask for, you can do it at any time. You change what you're thinking about. You know if you've made the change by the way you feel.

We have talked ourselves into believing that change is difficult and that it takes time. We THINK that change is difficult and that change takes time. Therefore, change IS difficult and it takes time.

We all have experiences in our lives when change was urgent; there was no time. The need was stated, the discussion occurred, the thinking about the need was done swiftly, the change occurred swiftly for those who thought it possible. The urgent change was the dominant thought; there was no thought about a long and difficult process. And so it happened. It's called transformation.

On the other hand, we set goals for one year, two years, five years, and long term. We think about those terms and things will often happen in those time frames and everyone is happy. But what if each goal became a dominant thought in our collective minds? The goal would be accomplished. I am certain of that.

If our thoughts were concentrated on not having bad language in our school, we would think about only good language; only acceptable language would be our expectation. We would not think about the possibility of bad language; we would make known our expectations to students. We would not accept a bad term and we would change it to an acceptable way of speaking.

We would have only positive expectations for our students. Our students would know what those expectations were because of our understanding of each other and our belief that we would have a more positive, happy learning place. We would talk about how we would do that. Anytime we had a negative thought, we would agree to change to a positive thought. Anytime we started to say something unacceptable, we would change our thought to an acceptable term or expression. I believe it is as simple as that.

But we make it difficult because just like the recovering alcoholic in Chapter 10, we start with all the "what ifs." The poet, T. S. Eliot had good advice: "Only those who risk going too far can possibly find out how far one can go."

I can think of so many experiences with student teachers, interns, and students in teacher education classes. "Well, that sounds really great, but what if...?" The minute the "what if" occurs, there is a transmission of thought that makes that thought a possibility. I have always suggested that the reason we don't try things is because we are afraid of all the things that might happen.

When we begin to fear and we think of that "what if" possibility, we have created that possibility. We will transmit that thought to our students; the thought will find like thoughts from students, and we have the "what if" occur. Then we are certain that our fears were justified. We have confirmed our disbeliefs. I am certain that had we transmitted only thoughts of belief, thoughts that were only those behaviors that we wanted, we would have attained them. Our positive thoughts would have found similar positive thoughts and more and more and the miracle would have happened.

Our thoughts become our self-fulfilling prophecies. We have all talked about self-fulfilling prophecies. What we need to understand is that our thoughts become our lives. Our classrooms become what we are thinking about. Our students behave in accordance with our thoughts that become our expectations. We continue to ask the question, "But are you saying I wanted my students to behave badly?" "Are you suggesting that I wanted that student to get angry?" The teacher or administrator continues to profess his/her desire for good behavior.

As you get under the surface, you find the fears and distrust. "Well, I would be naïve to think that Johnny could change overnight." "I have too much time with this kid not to worry about her language." As you discuss the situation, you find the thoughts that cause the students to continue their old behavior. There are fears and those fears are expressed as thoughts that are transmitted and received. The teacher is also a magnet. The minute there is a negative thought transmitted, that thought will attract like thoughts. It is a Law of the Universe. If you want to change the reception, the transmission must be changed.

I believe that it is that easy.

To simplify it even further, remember that you know what you're transmitting by the way that you feel. Some like to call this our inner compass. When you have a fearful thought, it is negative and you will feel that negativity. You cannot have that negative feeling and be thinking only positive thoughts. The laws of physics don't work that way. You cannot get the behavior you desire when you're fearful that you won't.

Yes, I have heard all about the role of parents, the role of the community, and the role of the multitudes. I know they are all factors. But I am talking about the immediate environment over which we have control. When we decide that we can't do much with Joey or Suzy because of the way they behave at home, we are thinking negative thoughts; we have already lost the battle. Those thoughts will be transmitted and we will be inviting the behaviors that we don't want. When we say it is difficult to control "these boys" right after they come from physical education, our transmission to the boys will be exactly that. That's what we will get. The laws of the universe are pure. You can attract only like thoughts and the consequent behaviors.

It is that simple.

It is easy for you to dismiss what I am saying. "But you don't know this bunch of hoodlums that I have in fourth period." "You've never experienced a class like this." "I don't think you understand the home this kid comes from." "I have this principal who just won't support me." "I get these students right after snack; they're loaded with sugar." "I understand this kid's behavior because he's a carbon copy of me."

You can supply your own dismissal statements. Dismissal statements contain negativity and excuses. They are thoughts that you transmit; they are received and you get exactly what you don't want but what you have asked for through your thoughts. We are in control of our thoughts, and we can change them at will. Why, then, do we continue to believe that change should be so difficult and take so long?

We have the tools that we need, but if we don't utilize the gifts that we have been given, the *secret* will never be ours. We will look and see the success of others and continue to see ourselves as victims. We will moan and groan about the students and parents that we have, when all we need to do is change what we are thinking to change our environment.

I have told students many times that I care that they are hungry or that they are tired. Whatever they have as an "excuse" is important to me, but it does not change my thoughts about them or what I expect in my class or the lunch period, or assembly or whatever. Our behavior together is explicitly expressed; the doubts and fears are not thought about, the excuses are not thought about; therefore, they cannot be transmitted. If they are not transmitted, they cannot be received.

The thoughts transmitted are thoughts of positive expectation, of love and compassion, not sympathy. The teacher's thoughts will attract like thoughts in the classroom, those will be added to the teachers and the positive and loving thoughts will overpower the negative thoughts. Positive thoughts are much more powerful than negative.

So many of the ideas, fads, and methods that have been introduced and championed are attempted explanations for the Law of Attraction. The idea of relevance has had staying power. Teachers have come to believe it's easier to teach material that has some relevance to the student. It seems like a natural. Why would we want to teach irrelevant information?

Unfortunately, most of the curriculum is prescribed and proscribed. Standards and accountability have taken over. Most states have developed standards in most or all of the disciplines teachers are expected to teach. Most states have developed tests to measure the progress of the students. Most have had many legislative sessions about accountability. Consequently, the relevance issue has often been subsumed as the "experts" of the discipline decide what is important for students to know.

In spite of the demands of the state and school districts, teachers still try to find ways to make material relevant to learners. They do this because they know that something that holds the interest, has some special meaning, or material that the student wants to know is a lot easier to teach. Life in the classroom is much more pleasant with the relevancy factor observed and implemented. Why is this so?

One of my student teachers was having a very difficult time teaching decimals and fractions. He announced to me that a particular class just didn't get it no matter how he tried to teach the material. I asked if I could try; he was more than happy to turn the class over to me. I knew that I had to find a way to make the material relevant to sixth-graders. I needed to add to the neuronal connections they had in place. I asked a few questions, mixed in a few math questions without expecting answers. I discovered that about half the class was interested in motorcycles. Aha! I thought. I will build math problems around motorcycles. There would be neurons on which I could build new concepts.

USING THE NEURONS

I constructed problems about the cost of the motorcycle. If a motorcycle costs $1,000 and you pay $100 per month, how long will it take you to pay for it? If you are buying it with your brother and each of you is paying half, how much is your share? If it is purchased with three friends or four friends, how much will your share be? I showed them on the chalkboard what they were doing; I put names to the processes. This is a fraction, a decimal, etc. I continued this for almost an hour, moving from simple questions to more complex problems.

The students answered them quickly and joyfully. They would answer and I would tell them how good they were with fraction problems. Or I would tell them they were exceptionally good with decimals. They were astounded and kept saying, "That's really a decimal problem?" or "Wow, that was an easy fraction problem. I didn't think I could do that."

How long did it take to change? Only as long as it took me to transmit positive thoughts about fractions and decimals and attract positive thoughts from the students. It was successful because I transmitted positive, happy thoughts and built on neuronal connections that existed. The Law of Attraction found other happy, positive thoughts, gathered them together and the miracle happened. The student teacher looked on with awe; these kids who couldn't do decimals and fractions were doing them in their heads with ease. The relevance of the questions changed the thoughts of the students to "can do" from "can't do." The change occurred because the students changed what they were thinking about decimals and fractions.

Several years ago, I spent several months home schooling my grandson who was eleven years old. He was having great difficulty with word/story problems in math. He had decided that he couldn't do them, just didn't understand how. I took the problems that he was unable to solve or didn't even try to solve and made all story problems about golf, keeping the exact same numbers and concepts. I just changed the houses and things to golf courses and the apples and oranges to golf balls.

His eyes sparkled; he handed me the paper on which he was going to write the answers and said, "I don't need this, Grandma; these problems are too easy." He proceeded to give me the answers. Why did this happen?

First, you need to know that golf was and is his passion. He had only happy, positive thoughts about golf, and he had neuronal connections built on golf. When he read the problem, he could connect with my thoughts—positive thoughts. He changed his thought patterns within seconds. The "relevancy" factor is better named the Law of Attraction. When I explained that they were the same story problems, his only response was, "Really, but they don't look the same; the golf problems were real. I didn't care how many apartment houses there were or how many apples Ned had in comparison to Joe." That response says more than most textbooks.

How could he have success while thinking negative thoughts? The two don't go together. Once he had positive thoughts he could succeed. He had neuronal patterns relative to golf on which he could build; they were established, usable neuronal connections. It was an easy "fix' because there was a base on which to build.

We have not been taught the simplicity of changing what we're thinking as a method to effect change in our classrooms. We have been told to be relevant; we have been told to be positive; we have been told to teach to learning styles and to cover all of the multiple intelligences. We have been told to change our behavior in many different ways. But we keep the same thoughts we have had and wonder why "all of our efforts don't work."

The simple fact is that in spite of new materials, new ideas, new methods, our minds are thinking the same thoughts, sending the same negative transmissions. Test yourself. Are you feeling happy? Or are you still thinking about your talk with the principal or the disagreeable drive you had on the way to school this morning?

The Universe does not get your transmissions mixed up. What you're thinking is what you send out. You may make all the excuses in the world, but when you test your guidance system—your feelings—you will find that your negative thoughts were there. If you want the results that you desire, you must change your thinking. ASK, BELIEVE, AND RECEIVE. If you do not believe and change your thoughts accordingly, you will not receive.

Change is as easy as that. I want to give one more powerful example.

When I was directing an Upward Bound program at the University of California, Riverside, the students kept coming to me and the tutors with a major problem—theft. They wanted us to solve the problems that stealing from each other caused the program and them personally.

We tried various approaches to the problem. We made more rules;

we tried to monitor personal property more closely. We threatened expulsion from the program, but the problem continued. A decision was made to have a retreat away from the university. There we would have the sole purpose of "solving" several problems. including the theft issue. We knew that there were a few students in the program who were proficient enough with this activity that they had regular "fences" to take care of the items they stole.

We arrived at the retreat in the beautiful California mountains. We went to work immediately setting up our "problem solving" sessions. The students were placed in groups with the younger and older kids mixed. (The program consisted of junior and senior high students.) The question was posed: How do we stop the stealing in our program? After time for discussion, we asked the groups to report on their "solutions."

The first suggestion from almost every group was to institute rules against stealing. I asked just one question in response. "Do you think this will stop the stealing?" They thought for just a minute and the answers were a resounding "No."

I told them to go back to their discussion; find a solution. After a few more minutes of discussion, they came with their next suggestion. The tutors and I were to monitor the situations more closely and punish the culprits. They obviously were not thinking about how they could stop the stealing, but rather how we could respond to it. There was a big problem. We didn't know who was doing it. Again, I posed just one question. "Do you think this will stop the stealing?" Again, there was a resounding "No."

They were asked to continue the discussions to find a solution. They realized that we did not intend to take the responsibility for their problem. We were asking them to solve their problem. This time the discussions were different. They were more subdued and serious. The next response came in a shorter time than we expected. There was a sense of joy and certainty in their response. "We have a solution! We have to stop stealing from each other." WOW! We all stood and looked at each other. We did not have to ask if that would solve the problem; it obviously would.

The next morning when they emerged from their sleeping quarters and we met on our way to breakfast, I literally had kids jumping on me, yelling, clapping their hands with such glee, and showing other incredible signs of joy as they explained what happened that night. They had left their radios, jewelry, valuables and billfolds out; they had placed things in the open that they felt the need to hide before. Everything was in place just as they had left it. Nothing had been stolen.

It was as easy as that. They had to do just one thing; they had to change the thought from stealing to not stealing. They had control over the situation. They, and we, had created and experienced an incredible power—the power of thought, the power of what we ask for, what we believe, and what we receive.

We can change. We just need to change our thoughts. It doesn't take time, or a meeting, or a conference. It can be instantaneous, just as fast as the thoughts are changed.

CHAPTER 12

CULTURE, CHOICE, AND CHANGE

When we contemplate change, when we mandate change, when we expect change we know that thinking has to change. The way we think about whatever we want to change has to change. In our classrooms, we expect our students to do something differently. We expect our colleagues to approach a challenge in a different way. Thinking has to change; new thoughts are required. This means that the choice to change has to be present. When a cultural belief precludes an opportunity from being a choice, a different dilemma exists.

To illustrate, I am using a very common expression. "You can be or do anything that you want." It appears to be possible. The roads seem to be clear. Opportunities seem to be present, but what if the culture instills other beliefs?

It is a phrase that I have heard so many times. The advice is more common, I believe, for girls than for boys. All one has to do is look around the world and check out the status of women in the culture to know that limited roles for women exist in almost all cultures. There is little to be gained to speak of the horrific practices in some cultures. We have been taught to "respect the culture." We are taught to "understand" the culture. When we speak of change, we are called names.

Fortunately, in America we have tired of the names and have pursued the path of rights for all. We have declared the right of all boys and girls to attend school to any level they wish to pursue. We have worked diligently to give all of our learners choices. But choice is an interesting concept. It suggests availability. To choose means that one has to BELIEVE that the option is available.

Now our sentence must read: You can be or do anything that you want and that you believe you can be or do.. And therein lies the *secret*. Ask, BELIEVE, and receive. The believing part is an a priori condition. The *secret* is the Law of Attraction. We attract what we believe, what we think.

For many years I have tried to explain to educators that making subjects/classes available doesn't mean that everyone in the school has the same choice available to them, the same availability. The choice, the availability, depends upon their thoughts about the subjects or classes. For many years, I looked at the paucity of female students in higher math and advanced sciences. Chemistry was often equally populated with girls and boys; physics might have one or two girls. The advanced math classes were largely boys. Yet they were on the books and available as far as most were concerned. Why did chemistry have more girls than physics? Girls needed chemistry to become nurses; they believed they could do it because it was required for the profession they believed they could do. Also, it was a matter of usefulness. The girls who were in physics and higher math classes believed that they could become engineers, doctors, architects.

When I was Dean of Women at the University of California, Riverside, in the mid-sixties, I saw clearly for the first time the disparagement of women relative to certain "male" professions. I experienced it myself when I was told by the Chancellor that I could not be Dean of Students because I was a woman.

Young women told me their situations. One young woman was denied a research assistant position because she would bother the young men in the labs. Another was denied a teaching assistant position in philosophy because pursuing a doctorate in philosophy was a waste of time for her; there would be no teaching positions at the university level for her when she finished. Once these young women knew that they had my ear and that I was willing to discuss issues with them, expressions of these kinds of limiting situations were a common occurrence.

Because I had not experienced gender bias and discrimination prior to my experiences at Riverside, my first thoughts were about possible shortcomings of the young women. How did they conduct themselves in the interview? What were the personality factors present that might be a problem? How could I help them attain their goals?

Unfortunately, as I made inquiries to the professors in charge, the department chairs, and the deans, I heard shocking news about the potential for women in philosophy and the uselessness of their applications for research assistantships. I received an education about gender bias and discrimination in a short time in a world where one would least expect bias—the university environment. These same university folks were most active in issues of race and ethnicity. They spoke, wrote papers, marched in demonstrations and made certain that equity was kept in the forefront of university affairs.

How could I have been so blind to the world around me? As I thought about it, I had not experienced it until I held university positions where I ventured into "the male domain," the positions that were for men only.

The *secret* is not available to you if you don't BELIEVE that it is. Belief is at the beginning; you must believe it to see it; you must believe it is available to you to think that you can have it. I cannot counsel you; I cannot serve your needs; I cannot aid you if I don't believe that the Law of Attraction is available. My thoughts become limiters; not enablers. I can only serve you when I make certain that my thoughts are positive, when my thoughts believe what they want to see.

MY EDUCATION

I knew I had much work to do. I started researching the issue; I talked to personnel directors. I talked to deans and department chairs. I started writing and speaking about my concerns. I discovered the nerve endings on the matter. I was amazed at the headlines and the reporting of my talks. I found the importance to students played out. More and more students came to see me to discuss their situations.

Students from UCLA came to Riverside and asked me to teach a course on "Women in Our Age" which was designed by women students; the university had a series of student designed courses dealing with student concerns. I was asked to speak more and more and more. It became an increasing research interest of mine.

One of my more remarkable experiences came when I was a candidate for California State Superintendent of Public Instruction in 1970.

At the first press conference, my first question was, "Are you running as a woman or an educator?"

I asked the reporter whether or not he had asked Julian Nava if he were running as a Mexican American or an educator, Wilson Riles whether he was running as a black or an educator, and Max Rafferty whether he was running as a man or an educator.

The reporter smiled and said, "I get it."

I tell you these anecdotes because they were a part of my education. I learned more clearly with each happening that availability does not mean choice is possible. If the desire is there but the belief is not, the thoughts of disbelief will attract more thoughts of disbelief and the desire is not met.

If we believe, or others tell us, that we cannot do something, or if we're told that women don't belong in that profession or job, it will remove the possibility from our mental list of desires. At least there is no clear path to our desires or dreams. Our muddled thoughts cannot attract anything but muddled wants. We cannot get what we want. Our thoughts manifest things, or they deny us our desires. The desire must be very clear in our thoughts for the desire to be manifested. Muddy thoughts will not produce clear transmission; the result will be the same as listening to two garbled messages from two transmissions.

When you are changing stations on your radio and you are between stations receiving a bit from each one, you have the same predicament as your own un-clear thoughts. "I would like to go to the dance, but I don't suppose anyone will ask me." "I really want to go to college, but no one in my family has gone to college." "I'm going to try for that job even though women don't do construction." The Universe is listening to two messages. You can attract only thoughts that are on the same frequency. Therefore, the thoughts must be clear and the frequency pure.

As a counselor, one of the most common statements I heard was, "I don't want to…" followed by a host of phrases: be a teacher; go to college; be in business with my folks; sit behind a desk all day; live where my parents do; be a druggie; be thirty when I take my first big trip; have my sister for a roommate; and a myriad more. Note that they are all negative. But the thought is still being sent out. The Law of Attraction will go to work because it receives the thought; it will attract what you don't want as easily as it attracts what you do want.

THE "DON'T WANT" EPIDEMIC

Often when pressed to declare what was wanted, there was not a clear answer. The answer heard most was: "I don't know." When students found that they were getting what they didn't want they were quite perplexed. I often told them that they needed to be clear about what they did want; what they didn't want could only help them if those thoughts pointed toward what they did want and if they started working on what they wanted. I was really telling them to change their thinking, change their thoughts. It would have been so much easier had I known then how to explain the full force of the Law of Attraction.

Authors have talked about how this scourge or epidemic of "don't wants" is kept alive. People keep this epidemic alive when they predominantly think speak, act, and focus on what they "don't want." The Law of Attraction doesn't hear any words but those sent out—your thoughts. The Universe can manifest only those thoughts that are sent and give you the things in those thoughts, negative or positive. When we think we are asking not to have "something," we are really asking to have it.

Young women were the most perplexed. So many of them wanted to be or do something different, something that their parents had not done. They wanted to climb a Mt. Everest that no woman had climbed. So often their dream thoughts had a trailer: "But I don't think my parents like the idea"; "but I don't know where I'm going to get the money"; "but my uncle doesn't think it's a good job for a woman"; "but it takes a long time to be a doctor"; "but I've never seen a woman do that job"; "but I don't think my parents will support me if I choose that major"; "my boss says I'm not strong enough"; "nice girls don't do those jobs"; and on went the "buts." Obviously, their negative thoughts could only bring them what they feared. Those were the like thoughts to be attracted.

It would have been so much more effective if I had been able to express the Law of Attraction in terms they could have understood. I always suggested that they talk to their folks, their uncle, their sister, their boss, but had I been able to get them to understand that they had to change their thoughts to only those things that they wanted, I believe they would have been more able to change their thinking. Had they been able to just drop the negative part of their thought, it could have made a world of difference in their lives.

Although I was highly successful as a counselor, I am saddened that at that time I did not have a full understanding of the potential in these universal laws. I was living them and using them but did not know the nuances, how to explain them to others.

AVAILABILITY WITHOUT CHOICE

While at the University of California, Riverside, I directed Upward Bound for a couple of years. The students in the program were great examples of availability without choice. The group was about twenty-five percent of each of four main groups—Black, Hispanic, Anglo, and Native American.

The students were mostly high school age with a few junior high. They were students who were academically low and many were students with behavior difficulties. In other words, they did not fit the mold of our schools. They had shown time and again that they could not or would not succeed in the school environment—local junior and senior high schools and an Indian school.

The Native American students were from many places in Arizona and New Mexico and represented several different tribes. The program was designed to make success in college possible for these youngsters.

JUST NOT WHAT YOU DID BEFORE

When we designed the curriculum, we planned to do different activities and models from what had been used in the public schools. It was obvious that the students weren't successful with the methods and models used there. Why would we repeat the things with which they had failed before? It was difficult to think exclusively in new ways, to give up old ways of doing things all at once. But we managed, with the help of the students, to bring new ways of looking at things to the students.

This is a good example of changing the way the students were thinking about schooling. They didn't know that they couldn't do the work since it was a different approach at which they had not failed. I am aware now that we were changing their negative thoughts about school to positive, fun ways of succeeding. We didn't expect the Native American kids to analyze and synthesize the world to pieces. We allowed them to view things as systems once they helped us learn that was "their way of looking at their world."

FACES OF LIMITATIONS

The Hispanic girls found themselves in cultural binds; they explained how difficult it was for them to think about going on when many of their families expected them to graduate high school and settle down, get married, and raise children. We had many meetings about the cultural patterns we were testing. How sad it was when we looked into the faces and hearts of these kids who had already placed so many limitations upon their lives and whose thoughts kept them well within these limitations.

We helped them succeed in areas where they had not placed limitations. They had no don'ts; they had not had anyone tell them they couldn't do those things. Anytime we ventured into methods, activities, models, or conversations where they had been mired before, the don'ts and doubts came back.

One day I told a wonderful Indian student from Arizona that I expected to see him in the Arizona Legislature after he finished college. He looked at me and said, "Don't you know we've been told at our school that we can only go to technical school in Oklahoma?" In another discussion about keeping commitments for tutoring I asked why they would say they would come and then not show up. One young man spoke up and said, "Don't you know we have lots of experience telling white man what he wants to hear?" I had offered to get someone else to work with them on this issue since I had not been successful. But they just smiled and told me they didn't want anyone else, not to worry, they would come.

They knew how much I cared about them and I believed this time they would do it; I had been completely honest with them. Every one of them showed up every time for every commitment from then on. People thought it was some kind of miracle. But it was only the secret of my asking and believing that they would. The *secret* in action produces miracles.

It would have been wonderful if I had been able to explain fully to our staff why it was happening, but at that point it seemed like a wonderful happening that you don't try to explain; you just enjoy it. But I suppose there were so many of these in my life that eventually I was compelled to write about it so others don't have to wait so long to understand.

I had an experience a couple of years ago that speaks volumes about limitations. I was turning in the final work for my home-schooled granddaughter. One of the teachers at the school was a student of mine more than 35 years ago. I was talking about the change in my granddaughter's behavior as a result of a positive, intentional attitude. The teacher started talking about how I had changed her life. She talked of the change in her life as a result of the talks that I had given the students about the social, cultural restrictions placed on girls and the attendant result—lack of choice for girls and women.

I wanted to make certain that these future teachers never placed those limitations on any of their students. The result was apparent; the insight had taken the cultural limitations from her soul. She changed her thinking about the matter, which changed her beliefs about who she was and what she could be. She has been teaching for 36 years now. We never know the extent of what a change in thinking can produce "down the road."

Cultural patterns and expectations mold our thinking and what we believe. Our beliefs are manifested in our behavior. To change means making a choice to think different thoughts. To think different thoughts, we must have real choice, free from cultural limitations that make an apparent opportunity unavailable.

One of the most remarkable facets of choice is that it can, in and of itself, produce change.

CHANGE FROM CHOICE

When people have choices, old institutions or ways of doing things can die because people who have choice no longer choose them or they change to encompass the new entity as their own and morph into a new entity. They see the handwriting on the wall when people stop choosing them. This is evident and easily recognized in the technology area. New inventions replace old ideas. If the old ideas and products don't change, they become obsolete and, "poof," they are gone. Unfortunately, in the education profession, there are internal self-preservation mechanisms in place that allow it to rest in its stagnation.

While at the University of Cincinnati, I had the great good fortune to work with an amazing colleague, Hendrik Gideonse, who was the dean. We came from opposite ends of the professional spectrum from the standpoint of our backgrounds and training. Because of the varied backgrounds, we had an incredible range of ideas and experiences from which we could draw. We spent considerable time talking about change and how to accomplish the changes we thought were necessary. As graduate dean of the College of Education and Home Economics, I found the conversations about the graduate programs exciting.

We knew that we wanted to see changes that would benefit the students. We decided to institute student self-designed graduate programs. Certainly this was not a choice in the culture of the college or anywhere in the university as far as we were aware. It was our belief that the potential success of these programs would alert the departments to the tenets of the programs in their areas that might need change.

This may seem like a dangerous route to some but we knew it would succeed. Our belief was strong that students would choose a program that allowed them freedom to pursue their dreams and their needs through their design rather than trying to fit their minds and souls into something that really didn't fit their needs. I recall a conversation with the graduate dean of the university who informed me that the program would fail because we would get only mediocre students. What he didn't realize was that we had set the academic standards very high; we had woven into the program facets contained in most graduate programs—Program Proposal, Faculty Committee with Chair, Candidacy, and Culminating Experience.

It was a much more difficult road for the student and required much more effort because it retained all the traditional steps and it required introspection, high expectation, creative thinking, problem solving, and self-motivation.. It is difficult to design your own program; it is easier academically to follow one designed by a department. Students were willing to follow the more difficult path to be able to design and follow their own program. They were not repeating things they already had; they were not forced into areas that had nothing to do with where they needed or wanted to go. It was truly amazing to see how difficult they made their programs; they didn't mind because they had their wagons hitched to their own star.

Recently I read the work of Clayton M. Christensen, who writes about how disruptive innovation will change the way the world learns. Actually we were using disruptive innovation as Christensen describes it. Christensen suggests that disruptive innovation does not come with a frontal attack on the existing institution or system, but rather by going around it. We did not have a name for what we thought it would take to change the system, but we knew it would take decades to change it with a "direct attack." We had both witnessed that for all of our careers. Creating choice, real and desired choice, is a way of innovative disruption. It happened even faster than either Hendrik or I dreamed that it could.

I left the University of Cincinnati to become the Dean of Education

125

at Oregon State University. Shortly after I left, the Self-Designed Program was not needed anymore. The departments had embraced the changes that were used in the innovation. By going around the departmental structure and offering a desirable choice, change was accomplished.

The diamond of choice has many facets to consider, and much brilliance to enjoy from the results..

CHAPTER 13

ASKING IN PICTURES—IMAGINEERING

Einstein has given us good advice: "Imagination is everything. It is the preview of life's coming attractions."

Sometimes the easiest way for us to experience something that we want is to imagine that it already exists. These are thoughts that are transmitted; by feeling the joy that accompanies the pretense, the thoughts continue to expand. What has been created is an environment of allowing. It is a celebration of the desire for the experience, not a thought about the lack of the experience. You are inviting the experience in. You are asking in a nonconventional manner, one that is allowing you to imagine its existence.

Picture exactly what you want, visualize the way things will look when you get what you want. The universe doesn't care whether you ask for a lot or a little. You may as well see your environment exactly as you would like it. Make it as perfect as you can. The response will be to whatever level you imagine. Be childlike again and pretend that you will get what you ask for.

Most of us are not good at pretending. Many of us have lost that capacity along the way. We have had the capacity to dream and pretend, to imagine, stolen from us. We started school and in so many cases, we learned that school was "real," that it was no place to pretend. We were not allowed to create playmates, or to pretend we got something for Christmas that we didn't get, or play with things that didn't exist. We had shiny new toys that were real, and no milk cartons strung together could possibly be a train when we had such a nice train to play with. As we search our memories to find niches that contain traces of pretending, we all could make our own list of times when we were told to "come back to the real world." But perhaps it's possible to get the feeling back. Perhaps you can remember how those moments were stolen from you and you can reclaim them again. Imagine, pretend, visualize, and experience the potential of the Law of Attraction.

Olympic athletes, championship golfers, hall-of-famers, and elite athletes describe the process of using their minds. They can create practice sessions without running a race or picking up a golf club. They can create the race in their mind and run the race in their mind.

The golfer pictures the course; she hears the sounds and smells the grass. She walks to the tee and hits the shot knowing that the picture in her mind is exactly the way she wants to hit the shot; she knows where the ball will land. She plays the game in her mind, shot by shot and putt by putt.

When she walks out to the course the next day to play the actual tournament, she can play the game just the way she pictured it—if she understands one basic fact. The mind does not differentiate between the picture and the game, between a visualized practice shot and a physically hit practice shot.

PICTURES, NOT WORDS

This is the importance of visualization. It is asking for what you want in pictures rather than physical action or words. The research is clear and sufficient. Studies abound on the science of the mind. Many have been done with athletes, but they have also been done in many other areas and circumstances. Visualization has been tested from the gym to prisoner of war situations. The power of visualization has been proven in circumstances from happy to dire. It is another set of proofs that thought is the controlling factor of presenting our wishes to the Universe of energy.

Just as the mental side of sports can create phenomenal performances, I believe that the mental side of the classroom can create phenomenal differences in its environment. The visualization of the environment we want will do wonders. It would be easy to scoff at the idea of picturing your ideal classroom. But if we don't picture such a loving and joyous place, how can we ever expect to attain it?

Maximizing the potential of the classroom must be a daily goal for any educator. That potential can be maximized only if the potential of each inhabitant is maximized. Therefore, the picture of the environment must be what we truly want, that enchanted place, a place where there is a positive picture of each person involved. We have tried to merge science and education with psychology and other sciences.

Educators have been reluctant to see how the science of the mind applies to them personally as well as to the persons with whom they interact. We see bright spots where teachers have "hit the gold." We see teachers and kids "in the zone" of learning. Their lives and their classrooms are examples of gold medal performances. But most educators have just not taken the lessons of the mental edge into their classrooms and their lives.

One very interesting thing about the Law of Attraction is that the response is to your thoughts, not what exists in your experience now. When you think about your classroom, you can imagine it exactly the way you want it. You can imagine the behavior, yours and the students, just the way you would like it to be.

Think about the difference between thinking about what you see and observe currently and what you would like to see and experience. The response will equal your thoughts. If you respond/think about what you are experiencing, that's what you will continue to experience. Often that is why the experience continues on the way it was. Remember, the response is to your thinking. And remember, you can tell whether or not you are on track to your pretending by the way you feel. If you're angry and frustrated because nothing has changed, look to your thoughts.

When your thinking is not much different from what it has been, when you continue to think in the same way that you always have, nothing can change. Moms Mabley suggested that, "If we always do what we always did, we always get what we always got." Ask the students to imagineer with you about their classroom.

When we say we would like a classroom with students who are attentive and engaged and happy, and we immediately suggest that the students we have are inattentive, disengaged and definitely don't want to be there, we set ourselves up for the latter. Those are the thoughts that we will transmit.

Suppose instead we sit quietly and we picture the classroom of our dreams. We see the sunlight and a clean and engaging room; we have brought some pleasant odors into the scene; we have fresh flowers;

we see smiling faces as they enter. Then we picture each student; we take in the smiles. We greet them and tell them how happy we are that they are happy today.

You are happy to be there; it's where you want to be at this moment. You have exciting things to do today. You know that the period or day will go by so rapidly that you will be sorry to see them leave. You smile and breathe deeply as you relax. And you think, "I am so lucky to have such a wonderful class. They bring joy into my life." You smile again, and walk toward the door. The bell rings and the students come. You can expect the same results if you can focus on the visualization. Remember, your brain doesn't know the difference between the visualization and the real happening.

Perhaps it won't happen all at once, but happen it will. If world-class athletes can attain transformations of their performances through visualization and other mental techniques, if Jack Nicklaus attributed 50 percent of his game to the mental/psychological aspects, and if doctors see miracle cures from imagery and visualization, why do we continue to stay mired in two worlds in our classrooms—one that we say we want and the one that we really are thinking about that we don't want? We are bound to get the latter because we are in every instance bound to receive the results that accrue from the Law of the Universe. We will attract the one we are thinking about. That is the law.

We can destroy the possibility of attaining our desired goal by continually talking ourselves out of it. "It would be OK if I didn't have these two boys"; "I wish I had this class a different period of the day"; "I hate teaching right after lunch"; "I need a different room"; "I seem to get the worst kids"; "my parents are really disinterested."

I wish, I wish, I wish. We can talk ourselves right into the things we don't want.

Instead, picture the two boys as great young men who want to be in your class; picture the class as being at the perfect time of the day; imagine your lunch adding energy to your being and making the period right after lunch special—everyone has just had a break. Picture your room as the perfect room, one where the students smile, the room is clean and where you've added plants and art. Look at the faces and visualize their smiles; picture the group as one of the nicest groups you've ever had.

Hour by hour, period by period, the pictures are the completion of a perfectly constructed tapestry. The background colors are woven together with the gold strands of the smiles and countenances of the students—a perfectly beautiful tapestry. You stand at the door and you see the background colors, and as each student walks in, you see the strands of gold that form the cohesive part of the picture. Each one is just right; each one adds the distinctive sheen necessary. And when it is all complete, everyone has the feeling of joy that comes from being part of a beautiful picture.

GET REAL

Now you may want to say, "Get real!" As I have talked with individuals and groups about visualization, the mental edge that positive thinking gives them, or when I talk about touching the souls, reaching the greatness in all students, the response is usually, "Wow," or "Get real." This is very real stuff that has been proven over and over. I use the sports analogies because it is something that most of us have witnessed. We have seen Kathy Rigby, Tiger Woods, Kobe Bryant, La Damian Tomlinson, Peyton Manning, and I could continue to name people in every sport that seem to play beyond reality. I could cite miracle cures in medicine; I could give you individual testimonials in many areas of our lives.

We have all experienced special times when we had a passion for something and felt the joy that followed peak experiences in that area. We listen with joy when our children have "unexplainable success." What happened? Great achievements happen from passion, from desire, not reality or will.

The performances and experiences matched the thoughts, the expectations. It is as we imagine. The imagination is a powerful force; creativity is powerful when allowed to be. If the desire is strong, strong mental pictures can be created. If the desire is weak, the picture will not be clear; it may float in and out of perception. Others may call it goal setting. The desire must be strong and clear. When you form the mental images of what you want, your brain goes into action. The research shows that there will be a firing of neurons that match the same neurons that would be activated if you were actually engaged in the activity you are picturing.

IMAGINEER YOUR CLASSROOM

So it is with the picture of your classroom. When you visualize clearly what you want, the same neurons will fire as those that actually fire when you are doing the things in the room to accomplish what you desire. If the picture becomes clouded, interfering thoughts enter, or the thoughts that produce the picture change when the first student walks in the door and you suddenly start worrying about the time of day, the way you feel, the boys who just walked in, what the students are wearing, your result will be disappointing.

When you relax and get out of the way and let the mind continue to take over, the picture will materialize from the visualization. You must keep the actual performance as positive and clear as the visualization. Your body will match the mind if the focus is the same. If the lens of the camera changes and the picture-taker focuses on a different picture, the camera will take that picture and that is the one that will be developed.

It is imperative that you keep the visualization positive and detailed. Your desires must be clear. You must focus the camera where you want the picture to be. Be clear about what you want. Remain clear about your desire, your goals.

When you are ready for the performance, when your students are approaching, keep the camera focused and the mental image the same. Keep the sense of the whole environment in focus. Remember the smells, the sounds of the voices, the joy and sense of being in a happy place. When your arm is bumped and the camera wants to take a different picture, remember the times when you took a bump on your camera arm, you held steady, kept the focus, and the picture was what you wanted. The success you wanted was the picture developed.

When you get another bump, tell yourself that you can do this; you can take this picture. You will develop the picture that you imagined. Even if the sun goes down, you will still stay true to the course of your dream; the change will only add interest to the picture. You will have the picture that you want. You will not have it any other way. Take a few deep breaths and refocus your camera. Remember the sounds of happy voices and the smiles on the faces, yours and the students. Assure yourself that you have pictured exactly what you want.

There are no errors. You ask, you believe, and you will receive. Visualize a classroom that has everything you have ever wanted your classroom to be. Describe the physical aspects of what you want. Describe the atmosphere, the occupants, and the nature of what will happen in this enchanting place.

The picture will be yours just as you visualized it. Mark Twain suggested, "You cannot depend upon your eyes when your imagination is not in focus." Focus your imagination.

CHAPTER 14

THE POWER OF FEELING GOOD

A powerful key to getting where you want to go, being who you want to be, receiving what you really want is feeling good. It sounds so simple. Just feel good. But it is quite simply true. We know that when we feel bad we are having bad thoughts and when we feel good that our thoughts are positive. We must understand that the power to the future we desire is in the NOW. It is not in the past or the future; it is in the now because that is the only thing that we can change. Our future might change as a result of changes in the now, but we cannot this minute change anything but the NOW. Within this NOW lies the future.

We want to change the environment in our classroom. We want it to be a happy place. We have bad feelings when we enter the place. "Oh, I wish I were someplace else," is the thought that enters our mind. That negative thought sets a person up for a bad day. You cannot have a good day somewhere wishing that you were somewhere else. The students will know and feel the same way. They may have come from another place where they enjoyed being, but it is absolutely certain that they will pick up your feelings and be unable to feel good. They may try. They may try to disengage from the negative environment. The teacher is the sender and the students will pick up the vibrations.

Will you change? If you can really hear the message, you can change as rapidly as you change your feelings. Look for something positive; think about something that brings a smile to your face; look for the smile that a happy student brings into your space; think about a place where you're always happy; think about someone special in your life whose presence brings you joy—bring up the image; go to a place in your mind that brings pleasant memories. Do anything that changes your emotional point of view immediately from negative to positive. You will not have to say anything to the students; your face, your body language, the messages from the vibrations that you transmit will tell them what is happening.

ONLY TWO

Remember, the "empty space" in the room is not empty! It is filled with positive or negative energy that we bring. It is one or the other; there are only those things that make us feel bad or those behaviors that make us feel good. There may be gradations of the feelings, but there are only those two.

We feel good or we feel bad. And what's even more wonderful is that we can change as rapidly as we feel the emotion. It is difficult to explain how important it is to understand this concept. It may seem difficult to implement; you can embrace only what you are ready to receive. But when you see through practice and results that you are the creator of your experiences, you will find the importance of your NOW.

We have an infinite source of energy available to us. We know that we have infinite energy to create, to do joyous tasks, to complete difficult assignments, and to spend hours doing something that we like to do. When we have passion about something or enthusiasm for a task, we have energy to burn. When we feel anger, frustration, revenge or any of a large array of negative emotions, we are tired and lethargic. We have little energy to do anything. The tasks are onerous and unpleasant. Why would we ever choose the latter behavior?

When we are feeling pleasure from a desire, we are in the process of allowing that desire to come to fruition. When we are feeling frustration or anger we are sending vibrations in the opposite direction of our desire. Negative emotions cause resistance to our desire and attract like emotions.

In the classroom, when we send out positive emotional vibrations we will automatically attract like emotions. They may not be as strong as we would like immediately, particularly if we have been sending out negative emotions. If we send out negative emotional vibrations, we will most assuredly get negative responses back. .

In all my experience in the classroom and in all of my visits to classrooms, I have never seen it otherwise. In those moments when I was puzzled about the behavior of students or of a teacher or other educational worker who seemed to be having a different response than usual, I would find that there was a difference in the emotional content of the situation. A usually happy, joyous teacher was "having a bad day."

When I felt ill or upset, I could explain to students that I would be trying very hard to send out only positive behaviors, but if I were unable to maintain, I hoped that they would understand. Often students would thank me for telling them because it allowed them to understand that their monitoring devices, their guidance systems would take care of it. In other words, when they started to get bad feelings, they could remember former positive days and smile.

138

IMMENSE LESSONS

In that moment they taught me immense lessons. They were able to create good feeling situations to control their emotions. They used their emotions to be the indicators of what was happening, and they would go to good feeling situations to change their emotions. They used the content of their emotions to be guides to the directions of their thoughts. Feeling bad meant bad thoughts; seek another direction for good thoughts. Feeling good meant good thoughts; stay on that course. The energy is positive. Imagine how much happiness this ability to change to better thoughts would bring to these people throughout their lives.

These young people had learned early that they were capable of directing their thoughts. When I told them that I was having difficulty functioning the way that I usually did, they could imagine what that might mean because we had discussed what their response might be to various behaviors on my part. They also had other teacher-student relationships in their background/experience.

They could imagine what could be and they could choose the path that would lead to what they wanted them to be. They chose to participate in what they wanted the class to be like rather than what they didn't want. As I look back on these experiences, I find them quite remarkable. I only wish that I could have explained to them just how remarkable their behavior was.

Sometimes students would tell me that they tried, but they had difficulty. I wish I would have known how to help them to feel better about their attempts. If only I could have explained to them that sometimes it may seem difficult to change dramatically in one day or a short period of time, but that their efforts were not lost, and if they continued they could make the change over a period of time. When they learned to change their thoughts, they would see immediate changes. Then they would realize that "time" was not the issue. Their ability to monitor and change their thoughts would bring them the change they desired.

It would have been helpful to them if I had asked them how they felt. What were their feelings as they tried to make the changes? I could have explained that they had a guidance system that was explicit and accurate—how they felt would tell them what their thoughts were. Then they could change their thoughts. They could look for a more positive statement and know the direction of their thoughts by the way they felt.

I could have told them how mature they were; they were aware of what they didn't want—a negative classroom. I wish I could have explained that when they were so aware of what they didn't want that they were not in alignment with what they did want. They were such willing beings that they were anxious to try to bring about the environment in which they felt good. They knew the difference and they wanted and were willing to work for one that allowed students to feel good.

I can only look back and wish that I had known more about the Law of Attraction. I believe that I was being positive and always had positive expectations. But if I had the experience and conceptual structure to tell them more about the strength and importance of feeling good, they would have understood the incredible power feeling good has. I could simply have told them, "If you don't feel good with the thoughts that you have, change your thoughts. When you feel good, you will know that your thoughts are on the right path."

If I were teaching now, I would have them think of several times in the last few days when they had bad/angry/frustrated feelings about a situation or a person. I would have asked them to briefly describe the situation. Then I would have them take the situation and think of something they could have done or thought at that time that would have changed the situation's negative feelings to positive ones.

Then we would have spent time discussing and understanding what happened.

They would have understood. We would have created a place where everyone wanted to be. No one would be saying, "I would rather be…

CHAPTER 15

BEING GRATEFUL

Being grateful is an important part of the *secret*. We ask, we believe, and we receive. Then we forget the very important part of being grateful. We may say we would rather give than to receive; it is more fun to give than to receive; we are uncomfortable when things are done for us. We at that point clearly acknowledge to the Universe and to all around us that we think we are not worthy of gifts and success. We are not worthy to be on the receiving end of kindness; therefore, it becomes difficult to be grateful. Or we might be on the other side of the spectrum and believe that what we receive is ours and we don't need to be grateful for what we already own and deserve. It's the "Entitlement Attitude."

Either position is deadly in our personal lives and just as deadly in our classrooms. This seems like such an obvious understanding. If it is so obvious, why do we see so little gratitude, so few expressions of gratitude in our classrooms? There seems to be the general perception on the part of most teachers that they do not need to be grateful when students do what is "required" or when students respond in "expected" ways.

"Students know what I expect. They know what they should do. Why should I be grateful for that?" is the usual response. There is this general feeling that nothing needs to be said when performance matches the expectations; that is what has been asked for.

I have often visited classrooms and have been amazed at how well the students are performing. They do assignments correctly and quickly. They are pleased with what they have produced. They eagerly turn in their work and look for some kind of acknowledgment. But often papers are collected and placed in a pile, or dismissed as a student collects the papers and places them in a pile on the teacher's desk.

Often students correct each other's work and generally fully inform their peers what the results are. Often there are comments about the student's work that are not friendly. It is a time for the personalities of the students to play out; many get great joy in seeing someone else fail or not be successful. For the student who has perfect papers or very good ones, there are often remarks of ridicule or snide comments, certainly not comments of gratitude for a "task well done."

NOT EVEN A SMILE

When supervising student teachers or interns or when evaluating teachers, I have been amazed at the responses I received when I pointed out that behaviors expected and received should be acknowledged. Teachers have often said they saw no reason to give accolades to students for behaving in ways that were normal and expected. I watched teachers ask for, cajole about, insist upon, threaten consequences if students didn't change their behaviors. When the behavior changed, nothing happened. The teacher didn't even smile.

"You had a wonderful change in behavior; why did you not acknowledge the accomplishment?" I would ask. The general response was mind-numbing. "They know what they're supposed to do. Why should I make a fuss about something they should be doing anyway?"

To be grateful is an important part of who we are and what we project to others. Being grateful gets us more of the things we desire. It is no different in the classroom. When we get a behavior that we desire, being grateful accomplishes so much to maintain the positive changes and to gain even greater changes.

Feeling grateful is not difficult. "Thank you for..." "What a great job you're doing." "I appreciate your efforts." "It is so helpful to us all when you..." There are hundreds of ways to be grateful. Teachers have lists of ways to say thank you and hints by the dozens to use.

But it doesn't take esoteric comments or lists to be grateful. It takes only a change of attitude. It starts with self. We cannot be grateful in the classroom if we haven't learned and practiced gratitude. Take a gratitude walk. Show gratitude for what you have. When you gain something you desire, be grateful. Be grateful! Be grateful! Be grateful!

In education we have called this positive reinforcement—a reward or something pleasant that is given for a positive behavior with the hope that the behavior will happen again. But an "M&M" or a star is quite different from words spoken from another person. An expression of gratitude from the heart of someone is much sweeter than a reward. A reward of the soul is lasting; positive vibrations between individuals or groups are lasting. Students will know as they feel the positive vibrations. There are no vibrations in stars or M&M's.

DELIBERATE INTENT

Learners are thinking and receiving vibrations every minute they're with us. If we want to do what is right and what is best, we will think only of the behavior that we want. We will create the environment, the atmosphere in our classrooms by deliberate intent. And then we will be grateful and express our gratitude with our words and with our nonverbal behavior. Students, particularly children, will know if we are faking. It is not possible to say one thing and be thinking another and expect the learner to believe what we are saying. It is the vibrations from our thoughts that will get through. Remember that we are transmitters.

There have been so many times when I have heard disappointment from teachers about the response they get to something they had said. The question that came next was, "Why didn't they get it? They just don't listen." Unfortunately, the teachers were transmitting other messages. Their face still had an angry expression from a talk with the principal. Their body language was that of an unhappy person. Their thoughts were not those of their spoken words. When these observations were presented, interesting results occurred. "Oh, my gosh. You're right; I was still very angry with what the principal told me this morning." "What am I supposed to do? Leave part of me that thinks out of the classroom?" Others denied the possibility completely.

The fact is, you cannot leave your thoughts out of the classroom, but you can change what you're thinking. That is what you must do. No matter what words come out of our mouths, it is our thoughts that control what vibrations are given to our students.

We can tell students how proud we are of their behavior, but if we're thinking, "Well, it's about time you shaped up," that's what they'll know. Their receiver is as true and accurate as our transmitter. They know when you are grateful because they can feel it.

Students come to school to learn; they want to be in a place where they can be happy. If the teacher is not creating a cheerful, joyful place, the students will feel it. If a teacher is clear about what she wants and is strong about those desires and is attentive only to those things she wants, those things will happen. But the positive thoughts cannot be mixed with any doubt. Any negative thought will throw static into the transmission. It will be garbled at best and the result will not be the same.

AN ATTITUDE ADJUSTMENT

Being grateful is an attitude adjustment for most of us. I thought about how my day would go as a teacher if I practiced an attitude of gratitude all day. I would step out of bed and say thanks for the day. I would be thankful for the great shower, the breakfast that sustains me, and the car I drive to work. I would walk into the building and say thanks for the job. I would express gratitude for my colleagues, the students, the parents, and all the helpers. As the students entered, I would be thankful that they were present; I would ask about those not present. I would be thankful that I have the capacity to teach, that I have all the books and material that I need. I would demonstrate an appreciation and passion about my subject area. I would be grateful for questions, for interactions, for successes, small or large. I would be grateful that I had the opportunity to do lunch duty; it would give me more time with the students in another setting. I would be

146

grateful for the teachers meeting; it gives me another opportunity to show my gratitude to my peers and administrator. I would make my usual calls to parents to express my gratitude for their children and their help.

No matter how we feel about a situation, there is always something we can find to be grateful for. I wonder how much more satisfying each day would be if we kept a gratitude journal starting with "I am alive." If we were to start our day with gratefulness when we open our eyes, when we put our first foot on the floor, when we feel the warm water of the shower, the first wonderful odors that emanate from anything we cook, the roof over our heads, the car we drive to work, or the bus we ride, the weather of the day, the beauty of the first flower in the spring or the first yellow leaf in the fall, our day could only be positive.

What would the day be like when we entered our school building if we said a thank you to those who made it possible? What a day the principal would have if all who came into the office in the morning expressed thankfulness for the job they are fortunate to have. Wow!

Next, it's about the reason for being in this place, a school, this hopefully enchanted place of learning. The students start arriving. They are all flavors you could imagine and they represent all hues of the rainbow. They are your tapestry, each a different thread in the weaving of the treasure before you. You tell each one how happy you are that (s)he is there and how happy you are to be there. Resistance melts away and any frowns that entered no longer feel welcome there.

THE MULTIPLIER

When you engage your students in conversation that tells them that you really care about who they are, that you want to hear about their dreams and passions, they relax and the experiences they come with can become enriched; new neurons can connect. Gratitude is an amazing happening. It always succeeds when it is true gratitude because it multiples its effects. Students learn that they receive more when they are grateful for what they have.

Gratitude is often misjudged. It is not the giver who needs thanks; it is the receiver who needs to express gratitude. It is in the recognition of the bounties already in hand that allows the understanding of being grateful for what is added. That is what our modeling of gratitude will teach the learners.

THE GRATITUDE JOURNAL

If I were in the classroom now, I would keep a gratitude journal. I would also have each student take a few seconds at the beginning of each class to write in their own gratitude journal. I would share my journal entry that expressed my gratitude about them. I know that the environment in that class would be transformed. Just as our expression of gratitude for what we have changes our world because we get more as a result of that expression. It would change the atmosphere in a classroom from what's wrong to emphasis on what's right.

The universal laws would bring us more of what is right and more of what we are grateful for. It would take a few seconds of time, but they would be the seconds normally wasted at the beginning of class when students are "getting settled." Students would be on task as they entered. Positive thoughts would be present in the rooms. This would help accelerate the match between the teacher's positive thoughts and the positive thoughts of the students. This classroom would be a great atmosphere for learning and teaching.

When we are grateful, we are thinking positively. We will see miracles happen. When we are grateful, we notice more things to be grateful for. Should we feel ingratitude creeping into our minds, we might want to take a "grateful walk" around our area. When we say thanks with every step, we will see more smiles, more joy, and more success. When we are grateful, we appreciate what's around us. If we want something more, we need to be grateful for what we have. If we think about what we don't have, we will get more of what we don't want. Guaranteed. It is a Law of the Universe.

Now is the first day of the rest of your grateful life.

CHAPTER 16

PLASTICITY OF THE BRAIN AND LEARNING

The brain can change itself.

This should be exciting news for those who teach. For those who struggle with students who are not learning or those who seem not to care about learning, this should be news to make those who teach and desire to learn smile. Scientists have now proved that the brain can change itself without medicine or without surgery. For so many years we have been told that once the neurons are lost that they are gone forever—no chance to change. Whether the treatment was simply to improve the functioning of the brain or to recover from problems, I was taught it would do no good because the brain anatomy was fixed. The injury or condition was permanent. Current research proves otherwise.

It was thought and taught that there were areas of the brain that did certain things and that was that. As areas of the brain were mapped, they were designated as fixed. There was great excitement when an area was identified for a certain function; scientists were mapping with finality. We were taught that the only change that would occur after childhood would be the decline with age. There was common belief in all circles that "senior moments" were natural, no matter how unwanted they might be. Is it any wonder why such an expectation became the horrible reality of so many generations? I recall so many times saying to myself, "This is not going to happen to me."

MEDDLING METAPHORS

It was common teaching in the sciences that a lack of development, an injury, or loss of brain cells was the end of the story. The cells would never develop, function after an injury, or develop new patterns of functioning. What a horrible decree to place on the human family.

The brain was thought to be like a machine: Machines don't replace their parts or create new pathways to carry on lost functions. Machines don't change or grow. In education, the machine metaphor continues to have dire consequences. When you add the computer metaphor of the brain being "hard-wired," you end up with the belief that the brain is wired once and if the wires become crossed, fouled up, or are destroyed, it is permanent.

As you read about the struggles that scientists had who were witnessing and studying different ways to look at brain functioning, you realize the finality with which the views were held. The "localizationists," those who believed that certain functions were in certain areas, saw the brain as a machine or computer, held sway. Those who thought differently were ridiculed, essentially told to not waste their time, or suggestions were made that their research was sloppy or impossible to believe.

Neuroscience history adds to the machine metaphor. In the 17th century, William Harvey discovered how the blood circulates and that the heart functions as a pump, a machine. Rene Descartes thought that the brain and the nervous system functioned like a pump, thinking that fluid moved through the nerves. It was later determined that not fluid but electrical impulses flowed through the nerves. Again,

151

these ideas led to the premise that the brain as machine was made up of parts, each functioning in a certain place and with a particular function. Therefore, when a part was broken, injured, or lost, nothing could be done. End of story.

We must change our thinking about learning disabilities, about the brain and injuries, and just generally change the way that we view the brain and learning. We must truly understand that the plasticity of the brain places additional responsibility upon us as teachers and school people; we become distinct and direct influences in learners' lives. Plasticity gives us opportunity and hope for change and adaptation in our teaching and learning. We now must change our thinking to the possibilities rather than the limitations.

We know that "miracles" have happened. The blind have gained sight; the paralyzed have walked; the mute have learned to speak. The ill have gained health, and people with learning disorders have learned. But we have generally written off these happenings as miracles or the exception. We now must come to the realization that the brain can change its structure and function. We must think in a different way about learning. Understanding the plasticity of the brain can change how we view learning and, therefore, we can change our thinking about what we now believe can or can't be done.

BLESSING OR CURSE

The plasticity can be a blessing and a curse. Plasticity allows us to make changes, but it also results in behaviors that become habitual and not too helpful. Once a behavior is established, it can become more difficult to make other changes. It is estimated that each neuron in the cerebral cortex has approximately 2,500 synapses. Over the years the brain grows as each neuron sends out branches: axons, which send information out, and dendrites, which take in information. This increases the number of synapses.

By the time an infant is two or three years old, the synapses have increased to 15,000 per neuron. It is estimated that this is about twice as many as an adult brain, which has lost synaptic connections, largely through synaptic pruning, which takes place when connections aren't used. Connections that are activated are preserved and made stronger. Neurons do not survive if they do not serve a purpose. As connections become stronger and stronger, it is easy to see why it is more difficult to make changes.

Educators become gardeners of learning. When students aren't learning, neurons become weak and are pruned, much the way bushes and trees are pruned. The plasticity of the brain allows it to adapt itself to its learning environment. If students "check out" and are not with the program, pruning takes place.

It is believed that this is what happens in adolescence when so many students don't find the information or material to be useful or stimulating. They don't use the incredible capacity of their brains, and the synaptic pruning starts. They literally keep losing synapses that they don't use, or the space is taken over by new stimuli, probably not those we desire. Those synapses that are used, often for behaviors that are not positive or wanted socially, become stronger. The pruning continues and as each year passes there is more likelihood of failure in the current educational system.

Since the brain adapts to its environment, the science of the brain must instruct us in the establishment of our classroom environments. Fortunately for us, the brain never stops adjusting to the environment; it always remains open to change. Therefore, we are always able to change an environment and achieve desired change. But the change cannot happen in the same environment that caused all the synaptic pruning to take place. You cannot solve the problem by doing the same things that caused the problem.

We have the ability to learn and acquire new knowledge and skills throughout our lives. We have the capacity to remember, short-term and long-term. The brain changes. The internal structure of the neuron changes, and there is an increase in the number of synapses between neurons. It has been suggested by many that the main activity of the brain is to change itself.

Scientists are also proving the polysensory nature of the brain. It has been proved that sensory areas of the brain can process electrical signals from more than one sense. Dr Norman Doidge's book, *The Brain That Changes Itself*, is a must read about plasticity. He describes in easily understood language the important nature of this polysensory characteristic of the brain.

It is very important to understand the research that tells us that there are no visual images, sounds, smells or feelings moving in our neuronal receptors. Rather, there is a universal kind of language spoken in our brain. Sensory receptors apparently can translate signals not just from one sense, but from any of the senses. They translate the energy sent to the brain into electrical patterns. This ability of the sensory receptors to process information from any of the senses gives us more information about the lack of specialization of areas as once thought. Doidge and others think there is kind of universal language in the brain with no special impulses for each of the senses

The homogeneous nature of these sensory receptors paints a very different picture of the processing nature of the brain from that which most of us were taught. This helps us to understand the plasticity potential of the brain. Because the brain is not as specialized as we once thought, we can have much more hope of change, of dealing with learning difficulties.

When we understand the concept of plasticity, it changes the way we must look at learning. When we change from the ideas of the finality of brain cells that die or are injured to the idea of plasticity, we change from compensating for the lost cells, working around the problem, to exercising and working with the lost function. Activities to stimulate the brain areas commonly weakened are quite different from compensation activities. To understand the difference, design five activities to stimulate the brain and five that might be activities used to compensate.

IMPLICATIONS FOR EDUCATION

The implications for education are enormous. Clearly, many children would benefit from a brain-based assessment to identify their weakened functions and a program designed to strengthen them—a far more productive approach than tutoring that simply repeats a lesson and leads to endless frustration. When "weak links in the chain" are strengthened, people gain access to skill development that was formerly blocked, and they feel enormously liberated.

If a brain-based assessment were done early when the neuroplasticity is the greatest, a program could be designed to strengthen the problem areas found; cerebral areas of the brain needed could be enhanced. Much frustration could be avoided if a child could have an opportunity to grow rather than wire into his/her brain that the work is too hard or he/she is not capable of doing it. The science leads any thinking person to the conclusion that an individually designed program is the answer to many learning problems once the brain assessment is done. The child could learn to love school rather than hate it, could experience success and not hardwire failure into the brain.

The brain is a "use it or lose it" phenomenon. We understand and believe that we lose the use of muscles we don't use. Why do we not believe this about the brain? Young children make progress with brain-based exercises more readily than older children or adults. As stated earlier, it is thought that the young brain has 50 percent more connections available among neurons with many more synapses possible. If not used, many connections "die off" during adolescence. Scientists call it "pruning back." This is the tragedy that our schools and culture have produced. Many attempts have been made to make curriculum relevant and meaningful, but if students aren't given opportunities compatible with their brain potential, the increased connections necessary for new learning will not occur.

This does not mean that older students cannot make gains. Stimulating the brain makes it grow. Enriched and stimulating environments produce more branches and increase the number of synaptic connections. Brain weight is increased as a result of enriched environments. The increased branches seem to cause the neurons to be farther apart which leads to increased brain size and volume. This has been proved in scientific experiments with animals. It has also been confirmed for people through postmortem examinations. It is true: Use it or lose it.

Michael Merzenich, a leading scientist in the area of brain plasticity, specializes in improving people's ability to think and perceive by "redesigning" the brain through the training of specific processing areas of the brain, or brain maps, with specific exercises. These areas are required to do more work and develop more connections.

Plasticity exists from the cradle to the grave and radical improvements in cognitive functioning—how we learn, think, perceive, and remember—are thought to be possible at any age. Some scientists believe that exercising the brain may be as useful as drugs to treat some diseases.

All of us, at one time or another in our classes and various learning places, have encountered learners who needed something more than we were doing. The concepts that govern the laws of brain plasticity that show us that the brain can be improved, and that the brain will adapt to what it needs, give us much hope. Learning can occur in many instances that may have seemed impossible; the structure of the brain that can change can provide greater capacity to learn.

LEARNING HOW TO LEARN

The brain is constantly learning how to learn. We are acting in concert with the ideas of plasticity when we help our learners "learn how to learn." Just as we provide exercise to other parts of the body, we must provide exercise to the brain if we want it to remain active and in learning, receiving mode. We must look at the brain as a living organism, constantly open to change.

Earlier scientists had done brain mapping. Dr. Wilder Penfield, a neurosurgeon, mapped the sensory and motor parts of the brain. doing much of the work during brain surgery on cancer and epileptic patients when they could be conscious during the surgery and respond. Others mapped language areas and motor areas. In earlier history, even phrenologists had made extensive maps of the skull. Penfield's maps shaped the view of the brain for generations.

Scientists believed that the brain couldn't change, and they thought, therefore, that the maps were fixed and universal. That is what most of us were taught. The maps of the brain were permanent and unchangeable. Late in the 1800s, the physicist Lord Kelvin stated. "Radio has no future. Heavier than air flying machines are impossible. X-rays will prove to be a hoax." Such certainty must not be in our thinking about the brain because when nothing is certain, anything is possible.

Scientists have proved that the maps were neither immutable nor fixed. There is evidence that the sizes and the borders of the maps varied from individual to individual and that they changed depending on how they were used. They realized that the competitive nature of the plasticity was a factor also. This means that when an area of the brain is not used, it will be invaded by whatever stimuli are presented. A brain map space must be used or it will be taken over by another use. This accounts for the fact that skills to be retained in a sport or music or other area must be kept through use. It must retain its space. If another stimulus is given over and over, it will replace the existing use of the space.

COMPETITIVE PLASTICITY

Competitive plasticity also helps us to understand why good early childhood education is important. We need to get it correct early; it needs to be right the first time. Plasticity also is instructive about why our bad habits are so difficult to break or why it is so daunting to "unlearn" something. The incorrect learning that exists or the bad habit has a competitive advantage. It is not just a matter of putting new things into the brain to replace the old. We can't just put one thing in and take one thing out. When we think of the brain as a container and learning as putting something in the container, we have given ourselves an image that distorts our perception of the brain.

When we learn a bad habit, it takes over a brain map, and each time we repeat it, it claims more control of that map and prevents the use of space for "good" habits. That is why "unlearning" is often a lot harder than learning. There is competition for space and it is allocated on the basis of use it or lose it.

The competitive nature of the brain maps is at once exciting and sobering. The considerations for education are monumental. The opportunity to get it right the first time becomes incredibly important. Every child must have a brain assessment and an individual program designed to meet the needs of that child. The cost is too great to have any notion at the early ages that the child cannot learn, that the child is slow or mentally challenged, or the myriad other labels and excuses we give and make about why children can't, won't, or don't learn.

END OF STORY OR...

When you have to move from the belief that functions in the brain have a location and that is the end of the story to the fact that brain maps can change and do, it is quite a large jump. "Unlearning" the nature of the brain that had been taught and believed for centuries by leading scientists is as difficult as all "unlearning" is. Imagine the frustration of scientists who realized the potential of brain plasticity for many uses but could not convince other scientists. As educators, we need to recognize the potential for learning when we consider the plasticity of the brain, learning we may have deemed impossible.

Now imagine the idea that new maps can form, can change their borders, and even disappear. Certainly the formation of new maps means that new connections have to be forming. Scientists have proposed that when something is learned neurons are linked in new ways. The belief is that when the neurons fire together certain chemical changes occur in both and the connection becomes stronger. It is believed that neurons that fire together are wired together, that is, new brain maps can be formed. In this paradigm of thinking, learning problems, strokes, or injuries could be helped. Getting neurons available to fire together and wire together can get results never thought possible. Synapses grow and become stronger with use.

AS WE PONDER

As we ponder all of these incredible happenings in the brain research of the last short while, we must soberly think about the immense changes possible for the creation of new kinds of learning environments. We must discard so many of our self-protective at-

160

titudes—attitudes that protect us from responsibility for the learning of every child. It's not the genes. It's not the lack of breakfast. It's not the neighbors. It's not the other hundreds of reasons we hear about why kids can't/don't learn. It's about us realizing that the brain can change. When we come to understand the plasticity of the brain and when we function as learners and teachers as if it were true, we change our lives and the lives of those that we touch.

We move into each day with a totally different mental attitude. We see opportunities, not problems. We see colleagues in the endeavor, not them vs. us. We immediately change a negative thought to a positive one. We understand that our thoughts are energy vibrations that affect us and all who receive them. Because we believe, others learn to believe and trust us. We are grateful when we see positive changes. We encourage all to have dreams.

We spend our time walking through open doors, rather than looking for closed doors. We see rays of sunshine in our environment rather than slits of darkness and despair. We ask for what we need and know that it will happen, rather than spend time on all the things we can't have and all the terrible things that might happen. It is a different world when we wake up. We see all the beauty, the magnificence of the hummingbird that flits past us, the fragrance of the morning breezes.

We start our day with gratefulness for the opportunities that we will find. We end our day with gratefulness and joy for the opportunities that we have had. Wow! And we find that we still have energy to do more.

And it is no wonder that the people whom we touched this day were blessed with our love and our compassion, our positive energy, our willingness to serve, and with the *secret* in the classroom.

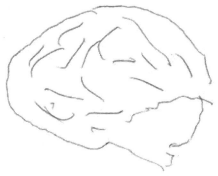

If I were teaching now, I would construct a mind map that I have about learning. When finished, I would document how my map affects one or more persons close to me—family, friends, or students. I would examine the map to determine what on the map I would like to keep and what I might want to change. After finishing the exercise, I would design the map that I want to have. I would include how the concepts of plasticity alter my map.

As I worked through the concepts in my map and as I applied them to the creation of the environment in my learning places, I would create my own proof. My brain could and did change.

CHAPTER 17

SERVING

When my son, Bob, was not yet four, he had a severe infection on his face. The doctor wanted to put him in the hospital in the contagion ward. As health coordinator in the schools at that time, I knew that there were some cases of polio there. I said absolutely not; we were not going to take a chance like that. We called our pediatrician in Seattle; he said to bring him in. Bob was wearing a natty tweed coat and hat. Dr. Fred didn't even bother to remove his hat. He took one look, took a scalpel and removed the crusty top that had formed on the infected area around his mouth and smothered it with ointment. He merely said, "We don't have much time." He was taken to the hospital and put in isolation. I was told that I would be given an opportunity to see him, but he must not see me. It could be disastrous if he saw me and started to cry for his mother.

I left the hospital feeling low, very low. My little boy was in the hospital in isolation, with splints on his little hands so he could not scratch his face. What was wrong with me? What a horrible mother I must be. If I had been with him all the time, perhaps he wouldn't have contracted this awful disease. It was my working that brought this on. I returned to the hospital as often as I could. It was painful to stand at the door and see my precious son with splints on, no ability to manipulate his hands to do much, and his little face with the horrible sore that one doctor had diagnosed as impetigo.

One day when I returned to the hospital for any news I might be able to gain and to get at least a peek at my son, a nurse met me.

"You work, don't you?" she said.

"Yes, I teach school," I replied. The feelings of guilt and despair swallowed me. I said to myself, "My God, I am so bad that it shows on the outside." I wanted to crawl under the linoleum floor. I was so busy feeling sorry for myself that I missed the soft, warm, comforting countenance with the smile to match.

"It's probably the thing that has saved his life," she said.

I looked at her with astonishment. "I don't understand," I said.

"It's apparent to all of us that he misses you but that he can live without you," she said. "Most children his age literally cry themselves to death when they can't be with their mother."

THE LESSON

It was a lesson for the ages. I knew in my heart that our job as parents was to help our children be the persons they are intended to be and to be people who care for us but who can live without us. It is our job, no matter what our relationship is with children, to be the adults who help them become successfully independent. It is only when they become independent that they can depend upon us without needing us. It was a lesson I used working as a counselor at the high school and community college levels. It is so easy as a counselor to create relationships that become needy. Unfortunately, they are created by needy people on both sides of the equation; however, it is our responsibility to fill needs but not create a need for the relationship to continue. In other words, the counselee needs you but can live without you.

It is true in every relationship in education—parenting, teaching, counseling, administering, bus driving, cooking, cleaning, keeping the grounds. Every interaction permits us to create continuing needs on the part of those we serve for our own satisfaction or meet their needs and set them free. They might miss us, but we have helped them to live without us.

This is not an easy task.

HELPING OR SERVING

It cannot be accomplished until we know who we are. When we try to be something we were not intended to be, we become needy. We are not living freely; we try to make up for it by living through others, by creating relationships where others need us. When we serve others, we do not create those needs. Our service speaks unto itself. We are fulfilling our own need when we "help" others. We are creating a situation where the other person owes us something.

You know when you have accomplished the difference, when you have served. You know because you have touched someone. You have not bound them

A former student described it well: "I cannot thank you enough for the difference you have made in my life. I love you and I want you to always be in my life. I already know that you will be in one form or another, because you have made an imprint on my life. I realize that I am one of many, many students whose lives you have touched.

But I hope I can make you understand what a difference you have made for me. I came home the first evening of class and I was so excited (just like I was a kid who loved her first day of school and could not wait to share her day with her loved ones). Well, my husband was asleep, my baby asleep next to him—the house was quiet. This gave me time to reflect, all alone, time I needed to absorb why I was so excited. I RESPARKED MY LIGHT. THANK YOU!"

Just think how many years this masters degree student had been in school. Just think how many times she had tried to light the flame of learning, but the spark was gone. We serve when we keep the spark alive, when we reach out and touch the soul where the spark is. We serve when we recognize when the spark is alive and we can help them find the igniting touch. We serve when we know that we cannot light the spark from the outside; it is an inside job. That's why it is imperative that we know that they are not ours, bound up with our ribbon, but that they are the sons and daughters of their own longing, their own lives, their own destiny.

When we know, we serve.

Serving is different from helping. Helping is based on inequality; it is not a relationship between equals. When you help you use your own strength to help those of lesser strength. When we help people we may inadvertently take away more than we can give them; we may diminish their self-esteem, their sense of worth, integrity and wholeness. Helping incurs debt. When you help someone, the person owes you one...When I help I have a feeling of satisfaction; when I serve I have a feeling of gratitude.

Serving is also different from fixing. When I fix a person I perceive them as broken, and their brokenness requires me to act. When I fix I do not see the wholeness in the other person or trust the integrity of the life in them. When I serve I see and trust that wholeness. Fixing is a form of judgment.

If helping is an experience of strength, fixing is an experience of mastery and expertise. Service, on the other hand, is an experience of mystery, surrender, and awe. A fixer has the illusion of being causal. A server knows that he or she is being used and has a willingness to be used in the service of something greater, something essentially unknown. We fix many different things in our lifetime, but when we serve we are always serving the same thing.

Everyone who has served through the history of time serves the wholeness and mystery in life. Service rests on the premises that the nature of life is sacred, that life is a holy mystery that has an unknown purpose. When we serve, we know that we belong to life and to that purpose. When we help we see life as weak; when we fix, we see life as broken. When we serve, we see life as whole. Fixing and helping are the basis of curing, but not of healing.

We can only serve that to which we are profoundly connected, that which we are willing to touch. This is Mother Teresa's basic message. We serve life not because it is broken but because it is holy.

Often in my graduate classes in education and often in personal conversations with educators, I have said that we truly teach when we touch the soul of another. We cannot serve if we think life is broken rather than holy. How many times have you heard a teacher say, "The lives of my children are holy and whole, and I must create an environment that preserves their wholeness and holiness"? Yes, how many times?

When we understand the nature and responsibility of serving, we will know and respect the wholeness and holiness of our learners.

CHAPTER 18

A LIFE IS CHANGED

Because learning changes the brain, any learning changes our lives!

How then, do we get the changes that we desire, the learning that we are striving for? How do we create an environment that alters people's lives for the better?

We are fortunate to be in education at a time when science is giving us answers to many of our questions if we but take advantage of the knowledge currently available. Most of us have read books on neuroscience, attended seminars on multiple intelligences, designed right- and left-brained activities, looked at what quantum physics has offered, yet we have not been engrossed in the biology of learning.

As a former biology teacher, I am stunned at what science has to offer. We should have guessed there was a lot there, since we are, after all, biological creatures. It has taken scientists who wanted to be better professors, researchers who were interested in the practicality of what they were doing, and educators who never gave up to lead us into new vistas, new horizons about learning.

If we start with the premise that learning is change because learning changes the brain, we have a starting line, a beginning point of reference. Somehow, we can start there, try to move to how learning changes the brain, and finally how we should teach to facilitate that process. It seems for centuries we have had it backwards: we taught,

169

they learned, or at least we hoped they did, but many of us took little responsibility when it didn't happen. What we need to admit is that learning took place, but it may not have been the learning that we had hoped for. It wasn't curriculum learning; they couldn't pass the test.

Our task is to understand the brain, the biology of learning, to enhance our ability to create learning environments that work. The brain changes with learning; it is not a hard-wired organ that stays static. We must know all that we can about environments in which brains change and grow, where learners are engaged and are committed to their learning and development.

Sometime ago, I was engaged in a discussion about meritorious behaviors of teachers. The topic was merit pay. The main issue was the presumption that we could not really define meritorious behaviors; they were too mushy to quantify in any way. I was challenged and went home and sat down at my computer. Within a rather short period of time, I had over 200 ideas about teaching that I thought qualified. As I view them now, they are actually about creating environments for learning.

I'm satisfied that No.1 is: **it is not about our teaching; it is about learning.**

Trying to connect the science about the brain as we know it to the environment we create and the practices of our work is the task. Measuring the practice, the technique, the activities, the lesson plan, the homework, the assessments, and even the way we look and the way our room feels against what we know about the brain and learning is the task. What then must the teacher do and be to facilitate positive learning?

THE TEACHER MUST MODEL AN ENVIRONMENT THAT MAKES STUDENT LEARNING PERSONAL.

It must matter; it must make a difference in students' lives. They need and want meaningful information and knowledge that makes sense. The learning must be connected to their world. Their starting line can only be from the knowledge base that they have. That is their world. Learning activities that require decision making on the part of the students will succeed. When students have control over their learning, the brain functions without fear. Fear inhibits learning. The being survives because of cognitive skills. Success is important and derives from learning.

This personal environment gives students choices. Constant attention is given to relate the activities to the real world of the learner and to the outside world. When these connections are made, motivation is high and boredom and resistance are low. Students engage willingly in this kind of an environment; it shows students how intelligent they are, not how intelligent the teacher is. There is a great deal of pleasure and joy in this environment.

Brains want to survive and grow; they do this by understanding their environment. They need sensory input, they try to avoid danger, and they search for pleasure. The brains of students need an environment of meaningful cognition, one free from danger and fear which means they need control to avoid these things. They need one in which they feel joy, pleasure, and excitement.

Making learning personal helps students feel that they are in control of their learning. This is a powerful tool in the arsenal of any teacher. When learners feel they have no control over what's happening, a red flag goes up in the brain. We cannot force the learner to learn, the brain to learn. When that red flag of no control goes up, the brain shifts into a fear and danger mode and makes the decision to opt out or fight for control. Often the result is a power struggle between student(s) and teacher.

One of the ways to make teaching easier is to find out what the students care about, what they want, and what they like. Very few learning environments are set up with these criteria in mind. They are structured around a curriculum, a discipline, a set of standards. The assumption is that these are the important things to learn. That may well be from the perspective of the adults designing the curriculum. But it will be very difficult to get the students to buy into that perspective if they don't want to learn what we have, if they see no use for it in their lives, and it doesn't matter to them personally.

To accomplish this personal learning environment, students need Individual Learning Plans. The use of current technology available for assessment and for following the needs and growth of learners makes ILP's possible for all learners. Students can understand and follow their learning desires and needs and can help the teachers accomplish curriculum goals. All the aids available make Individual Learning Plans a real and necessary possibility.

TEACHERS NEED MORE KNOWLEDGE OF THE BRAIN, THE "TOOL" MOST USED IN THEIR PROFESSIONS BY THEM AND THEIR LEARNERS.

It is time that educators become more familiar with at least some of the most important and rudimentary knowledge that would inform their decisions about their relationships and their practices.

To know that the amygdala is the region generally related to fear and anger and to know something of its functioning seems useful information. The experiences of a student will be filtered through this structure of cells the size and shape of an almond. Knowing this, how we plan our environment and how we practice our profession seem paramount.

Consider that all experiences in your charge will be monitored and most likely first by the amygdala of each student. These concrete happenings will be "checked out" by the learner for any sense of fear, any sense of danger, any sense of "what's happening is not right for me." When these emotions are present, the amygdala becomes more active and sorts out the meaning of the situation before anything happens cognitively. There is a constant vigilance of this part of the brain to all the activity being experienced; it is a survival mechanism.

When students are fearful and feel "in danger," the amygdala doesn't act alone. The adrenal glands produce adrenaline into the bloodstream; the physical action is fight or flight. Either reaction is a disaster for a learner when pursuing cognitive tasks that occur in the frontal cortex of the brain. The adrenaline tends to inhibit activity in that area. Reasoning and judgment are diminished. The learner drops out or fights for control of the situation and the teacher feels great frustration. Learning is not facilitated in this environment.

Survival is partly a search for joy and pleasure. Science suggests that positive emotions are centered in non-cortical clusters of cells. Pleasure is also an emotion of survival. Our brain seeks pleasure rather than pain, love rather than hate, success rather than failure, and fulfillment rather than emptiness.

Educators must realize that emotion walks into the classroom with the learner. It will be present whether or not we plan for it; best that we plan to garner the pleasant emotions and work with them in our learning environment.

We all find it difficult to think and do cognitive work when we feel negative emotions, when we are afraid, feel danger, or feel that we have no control over our educational well-being. Therefore, we must understand that learners' brains react in these ways.

We can no longer be oblivious to the science available to us. When we understand how and where and when cognitive work occurs and when the brain shuts it down for more basic needs of survival, we will look to ourselves, not the learners, for the answers to much abysmal classroom performance.

Pleasure is linked to motion and action. Games and play are generally linked to pleasurable emotions. Different kinds of music can create totally different emotions. Eating and engaging in conversations such as discussions and various kinds of groups can be very fruitful, positive emotional experiences. Learners will respond to action and movement. Many research studies have been done on the positive effects of music on academic achievement. When we are engaged in an emotional event, we often say we are "moved" by the experience. Often our language expresses the gist of positive and negative emotions.

Our bodies are a symphony of connections, a system of wiring between the various centers of the brain. Some run in both directions while others run only in one direction. Scientists believe there are more connections from the amygdala to the cortex than there are from the cortex to the amygdala. Scientists suggest that emotions tend to rule cognition and will be the dominant force when the two are competing. While we can have many feelings at once, the stronger ones will win. The attention required for cognitive activity, thinking and reasoning, will be absent in the presence of an environment of fear and perceived danger. Remember. danger can be a feeling of not having any control, not being interested, or not feeling any importance or connection to the situation.

In essence, what learning takes place depends upon how learners feel.

A SUCCESSFUL TEACHER WILL LEARN WHAT STUDENTS KNOW WHEN THEY ARRIVE.

A large part of what students feel is filtered through what they know. The brain enters the learning environment with neuronal connections in place. These connections are the starting line for subsequent learning. All learning starts from these points. The student can only make sense of what is presented if there is some connection that can be made, that is, if a neuronal path present in the student's brain can connect with the new learning to make a new path.

The number of neurons and connections is staggering. The brain has 10,000 connections for each of its approximate 100 billion neurons. Imagine the power and magnitude of many times more connections in our brains than there are cells in our bodies. When we learn something there is a neuronal network. It is there in a student's brain. Teachers can't just decide to ignore what is a fact. The student comes with these networks in place. Knowing this, the teacher needs to understand how to build on these existing networks.

Again we have a starting line. Use what the student brings. This is a biological necessity, not a discardable piece of pedagogy.

THE NEURONAL NETWORKS THAT EXIST ARE THE RESULT OF STUDENTS' EXPERIENCES. THEY ARE THE BIOLOGICAL RESULTS OF THEIR LIVING. TEACHERS MUST DISCOVER WHAT THESE LIFE EXPERIENCES ARE IF THEY ARE TO USE THEM EFFECTIVELY TO BUILD NEW NETWORKS.

Our starting line is where they are, not where we are. The idea that we present and they learn and if they don't, too bad, disregards important biological and psychological facts.

In addition, we disregard emotional issues with learners. When we do this they think what they know is not important and unworthy of respect. This brings emotional pain and stress. When we are not interested in what learners know and what they bring, they think we are not interested in them. They think we don't care. This is often perceived as nonacceptance.

We will find willing learners when we find out what they know and honor what they bring. When we ignore their life experiences, their existing neuronal networks, we miss an opportunity to build on their existing knowledge to create new paths. They have had lives before they came to us; we cannot pretend that we have "blank slates" or empty vessels in which to pour our curriculum.

Most of these neuronal connections are strong and we cannot erase them easily. Teachers may want to change some things that are harmful or work on habits that are not helpful to learners. But understanding the biological nature of neuronal connections and life experiences makes us careful of what we do and say.

When we try to "fix" the ideas and perceptions of our students, we generally have forgotten the basic premise of this section. Learners come with neuronal networks in place that are the sum of their experiences. They may not be smooth; they may have some strange pathways and some detours, but they are what we have to deal with. It is all that we have to build on; it is the sum total of neuronal pathways that exist, but that have infinite possibilities. It is those possibilities upon which we should make our curriculum and build our strategies. Knowing what they care about, what they believe, what their passions are, and particularly where their successes lie, can be the compass for our journey with them.

It might be helpful to imagine that the neuronal networks of a student look much like mind maps or pictures of their experiences. When we teach without knowing anything about our students and their mind maps, there is a strong possibility that we will not add clarity to their picture, but rather confusion in the networks. When blank faces occur, when students start opting out of the happenings, when little interest is evident, even when students disrupt to stop what's occurring, we might want to think about the mind map neuronal networks that are in a state of confusion.

Remember, we must know more about prior knowledge. Whatever we are teaching has to make sense; we have to cross a bridge to where they are if we are not on the same path. We have to understand that we have to connect with what they already know. We can do that best with concrete examples to match the concrete nature of their networks. We need to honor their prior knowledge as a bonus for us; it gives us a starting line for our teaching. Using the neuronal networks of the learner makes them stronger. This gives us a base for new material to establish new networks. As the old and the new fire together, they become wired together and the connections are made. It is upon this combination of the new and the old that we can build.

TEACHERS NEED TO BE CREATIVE TO FIND THE EXISTING NEURONAL NETWORKS.

When presenting new material, ask students to brainstorm about what the topic brings to mind. Find the words, the phrases and ideas that come to their minds. This will give concrete ideas on which the teacher and students can connect the old and the new. Explanations to students about how the old and the new connect to form new networks could help them to understand the process and become more committed to it.

Rather than be bored or uninterested, they know at once that their prior knowledge is being honored, and they also will feel safe, which allows them to function in positive ways. Giving support to what exists in the learner's brain creates not only an environment that is helpful to the learners, but also one that gives the teacher valuable information upon which the foundations for future learning can take place.

A question arises when the teacher discovers that information in current neuronal networks is clearly erroneous. When clarity of error is established in the teacher's mind, not perception of error, emphasis should be placed on the correct information by repeating the correct information, operation, or concept. By continuing to cause the correct neuronal networks to fire, the erroneous networks will weaken. If emphasis is placed on the "wrong idea," it will cause those networks to continue to be used. Ask for what you want, not what you don't want. Sometimes the networks are just incomplete.

Sometimes it is possible to connect "wrong ideas" with the correct or desired ones in unique ways. Helping students to use creative tools like metaphors, similes, and analogies can often give the teacher hints about concrete concepts that exist in networks of ideas. For instance, when a concept is wrong, have the students build a mind map with the "wrong" concept or word in the center. Or ask students to supply metaphors or other tools. When teachers use these tools, students often will be able to connect with the ideas or create their own metaphors that add concreteness and the possibility of connecting the old with the new. Let the brain tell us what it knows.

TEACHERS MUST MODEL A WILLINGNESS TO TAKE RISKS AND MUST ASK LEARNERS TO TAKE RISKS TO LEARN.

If teachers are to discover prior knowledge they must learn to accept different answers. They must learn to look for different routes to the knowledge. The leader must assume risks on behalf of the learners. If the teacher is afraid that the principal is watching or that the students might think he doesn't know something, there will be little risk taking.

When helping the students make new connections they must be allowed to make mistakes that will lead to new connections or a discarding of the old ideas; they must be allowed to take the road to independent thinking.

When we ask them to explore their ideas and assumptions, we have to be ready for different answers, new ideas, and ways to solve presented problems. When students question their assumptions or the assumptions of the teacher, they should be encouraged to present their thinking. Teachers should question the assumptions they hold in order to become better listeners for new ideas. Also, they should help students question their assumptions so they might become better listeners.

Teachers can learn much when they ask the student questions about how they learn and ask students to help them find the answers. Teachers often see this as risky business; they are afraid that students will question their competency or confidence. If the effort is an honest one, the students will respond with openness and support. Support flows in two directions.

It is critical to understand that students will choose risk over certainty if the consequences of the choice are more satisfying. When the teacher models a fondness for questions over answers, the students will feel safe to follow. Remember the amygdala. Feeling safe and feeling control over their being will allow the other parts of the brain to function to create new connections and exciting learning.

All the experiences will be filtered through that organ, and the positive emotions generated will allow great things to happen. Students know that it is safe. We do not take risks unless we feel safe. That is a biological fact.

We also know that students will pick up the feelings and attitudes of the teacher; the vibrations of the thoughts of the teacher will be there. They will know when it is safe because the teacher is willing to take risks. Saying it is a safe place doesn't make it safe. Actions make it safe. When the actions are right, the amygdala turns on the green light.

When I was teaching physical education in Klamath Falls, Oregon, I found myself in a wonderful but troubling situation. It was wonderful because students were constantly seeking personal information and asking for answers to questions they had in their teen lives. It was troubling because I found myself trying to accommodate the ever-cascading flood of questions and also get to my classes on time, which is what I expected of them.

I pondered the situation for some time and finally decided to engage the students in seeking help with the dilemma. We set aside a day to talk together. At the beginning of each class I outlined the situation and suggested some ideas that might help and asked them to make suggestions, to alter or add to those I had presented. I explained that there was a body of knowledge and sets of skills and attitudes for which I was held responsible. It was called our Physical Education curriculum.

My proposal, my "deal," was that if we could accomplish in four days of the week what I had planned for five, Friday could be theirs to discuss all the topics they had been seeking information about and all the questions they had been asking me.

What happened was totally amazing. Smiles appeared, bodies became animated and engaged, eyes were bright and eager. They were looking to each other and nodding "yes" with obvious anticipation and joy. I had six classes and all responded the same way.

"Yes, we want to do this! Can we really have Friday?" was the response.

What happened in the four days of class was incredible. My classes had always been active and productive, but to see these students respond with the energy and commitment that they did was a mind-opening happening for all of us, especially me. They not only fulfilled the expectations for the five days in four, but were always asking to go beyond. The commitment to each other was beautiful. Some were surprised at how much they enjoyed and liked their class. Everyone, including the principal, who watched our groups, was amazed and I think confounded. The principal asked me what threats or rules I had imposed to get such participation.

To the contrary. The biology of learning is very practical. I had given them some control over their experience, they were committed to each other as a community of learners, and there was no need for "fight or flight." The amygdala was happy; there was no need for fear. I was honoring the neuronal connections that existed. They are a physical reality.

The physiological reality of the amygdala is that there are more pathways, more connections that lead from the amygdala to the cortex of the brain than connections that lead in the other direction. This gives us a hint that emotions will influence our thinking more than cognition. Feelings always affect our thinking. It is a competition that goes on in the brain all the time. The strongest will win.

UNDERSTANDING HOW TO HELP STUDENTS CREATE RELATIONSHIPS BETWEEN DISCIPLINES AND IDEAS IS A POWERFUL TOOL IN TEACHING.

When the teacher models natural and unusual relationships between ideas and disciplines, students create new neuronal networks or can build on existing networks. Modeling of insights between seemingly unrelated events with the use of metaphors and stories becomes a powerful learning tool.

We know the power of parables if we have any knowledge of the teachings of one of the great teachers, Jesus Christ. We know that stories have been passed from generation to generation or have been created by people as they move through their experiences. Analogies and similes are likewise powerful learning aids.

Students understand a concept when their neuronal networks map some form of concrete relationships that give them physical structure to the concept. New networks are formed that progress from the concrete to the abstract. Often creating relationships can add to an incomplete neuronal network and learning can progress. Not only should the teacher use these strategies, but teachers should have students create their own metaphors, analogies, and stories. These student creations help the teacher to understand the concept better and aids in examples of new ways to describe relationships.

TEACHERS MUST ENGAGE AND ASK STUDENTS TO BE INVOLVED IN THE LEARNING AND TEACHING PROCESS.

Teachers need to give students choices about what activities will help them learn concepts and ideas. Students need to know that the teacher expects all students to learn. The world of ideas is opened up to all students and they all are helped to believe that they are capable of great things.

Ask them to create stories and metaphors. Ask them what they think about an assignment. If an atmosphere of trust, integrity, and respect has been created, an atmosphere where the teacher is not dogmatic, but listens, students will be honest and creative in their responses and suggestions.

A nurturing atmosphere is required for all to grow; there can be no room for the seeds of doubt to take root. There is no room for suspicion and fear when we ask students to bring and use what they know and when we use and respect what they bring to involve them in their learning.

WHEN TEACHERS MODEL, EXPECT, AND ASK FOR HIGHER LEVELS OF THINKING AND PROBLEM SOLVING, THE LEARNING IS ELECTRIC.

Modeling requires asking questions that have no immediate answers, keeping ideas floating around that require enhancement, and ideas that require the students to walk away and say, "I'll have to think about that." There is always a balance about the content and how to think about that content. All tasks require higher levels of thinking.

There is an expectation that students bring capacity to think at higher levels; they have been given gifts that must be found if they are not evident at first. There may be unused neurons and synapses, and there may be ones that are quiet or even have different or "wrong" connections from their experiences. There may be incomplete knowledge and neurons and synapses that need to be used and strengthened.

The teacher must model how to be intellectually active. There is an attitude of problem solving, of wonder and excitement as the search for deeper meaning and relationship to their lives is present in their learning.

THE TEACHER MUST MODEL THE BEHAVIOR THAT TELLS THE STUDENTS THAT SHE BELIEVES THERE IS NO LIMIT TO KNOWLEDGE.

In an atmosphere of infinite possibility and infinite opportunity, there is a lack of tolerance for finite answers to human development, ways of knowing and ways of doing. The environment is geared to exploring the edge of knowledge and beliefs in science and other disciplines.

The teacher appreciates oppositional or creative thinking and is not annoyed by this behavior. The learners know and feel that it is allowed and expected. Help is given to students to think the improbable for they cannot do the impossible if they are not allowed to think the improbable, yes even the invisible.

This teacher, who is a learner, never becomes victim to his or her own experience or knowledge that might allow a new idea to pass by. Remembering the potential of each student and the synergy possible from the group should keep the boundaries of learning open.

Remembering the immense number of neurons available must remind us as teachers and learners that we must learn more about how to make those neurons fire, how to use the bounty of the brain to create new and exciting pathways for students to follow.

TEACHERS WHO MODEL CREATIVE ENDEAVORS AND BEHAVIORS CONSTANTLY WILL CREATE AN ENVIRONMENT WHERE THE LEARNER CAN MAKE THE CONNECTIONS TO USE EXISTING SYNAPSES.

Creative thinking and creative behavior is the mode of operation; it is not just a happening.

Whether trying to maximize the learning styles or the various intelligences of the students, teachers must engage students in the subject matter in original ways; it is a commitment to convey the material in the best way possible. Creative assignments and assessments are designed and new theories are proposed.

Students can become a scientist or historical figure, invent their own fuel system, design simple perpetual motion machines, think about the things that people have invented or are happening when people said it was impossible. The teacher does not develop concretized attitudes and habits.

Learning in this environment is not a game played on a field or court with prescribed dimensions and prescribed rules.

There is a demonstration of a wide use of materials and ideas. The teacher does not expect or demand conformity except when needed to enhance learning or for safety. Even then there is listening to students with the third ear. The teacher allows learners to draw outside the lines and think outside the box. The teacher models a tolerance for ambiguity and expects that behavior from the student.

Ideas are respected and heard. Students are expected to listen and test their assumptions. The environment encourages students with new, different, creative ideas to persevere in the face of resistance they will encounter and the treatment that might ensue for being different, for thinking outside of the comfort zone of others.

In this enchanted place they will feel the joy of thinking outside their own comfort zone. They will live in an environment of wonder and excitement.

These are procedures and behaviors that create an environment for the student to use what he came to the class with, to find the connections that make new learning possible and exciting. It is a place where new synapses can be formed, and where the amygdala can rest. The student feels safe and energized.

STUDENTS RESPOND TO TEACHERS WHEN THEIR BEHAVIOR DEMONSTRATES COMMITMENT.

Teacher behavior in classrooms ranges from apathy to commitment. Some are compliant; they do what they absolutely have to do to get by. Others consider themselves "willing soldiers." They do what they are told to do and consider themselves good employees. But the teacher who is committed to teaching and learning behaves in the classroom in ways that convince students that what is being taught matters. This teacher models behaviors that demonstrate the belief that the purpose of education is more than gathering facts and gaining skills that happen to be in the subject. She models behaviors that demonstrate the value of all the disciplines, all the subjects.

The professional identity of this teacher is built on student learning, rather than subject matter. She is joyfully engaged in the act of teaching as an act of learning. She truly believes that all in the environment are both teachers and learners. She treats students with love and respect, compassion and patience. This is an environment of caring and warmth. She models a sense of gratitude for the opportunity to serve and learn, for all the things that go right and a sense of patience and humility when things need to be changed.

She expects and models behaviors that create an environment that is a safe, lively, animated, and desirable place to be. When the behaviors are present, they are noticed and accepted with gratitude.

An environment created by teachers who are committed to their learning and the learning of students and who create a community of learners is very different from one where teacher and students are compliant, just following the curriculum, standards, and policies set forth in manuals, documents, and directives.

Here the teacher models attitudes that indicate that the fate of the learner and the future rest with him. He generates enthusiasm for learning through personal involvement in the subject matter and exhibits skill in teaching. He brings passion about his personal learning into the learning situation every day by modeling an exceptional devotion to learning. There is passion about the subject that he is teaching. He understands the significance of the work in which all learners are engaged.

This teacher learns to negotiate with the authorities to preserve learning opportunities for students that might stray from the "curriculum." He demonstrates on a daily basis what he stands for.

There is collegiality in this environment. Students, teachers, administrators and staff participate in creating a shared vision and clear mission statement for the school. In this environment it is clear to all what is expected. It is also clear from the vision statement that no excuse for not learning will be accepted or tolerated. Everyone is committed to making it happen. All are committed to doing whatever it takes to make it happen. This teacher works with colleagues to soften or even abandon the boundaries of disciplines in favor of using and teaching knowledge when it is pertinent rather than when it is scheduled or convenient.

The commitment creates an environment where students never ask, "Why am I doing this?" They see the ties to their personal needs and knowledge base. They see the passion, energy, the investment of personal capital, the dedication, and the commitment to learning of their teacher. They willingly join in such an effort.
A LIFE IS CHANGED WHEN TEACHERS HONOR LEARNING AS LIFE-ALTERING EXPERIENCES.

The teacher who believes that she touches the heart and soul of each learner with each encounter in either a negative or positive way will create an environment based on that understanding. She understands that the multitude of decisions made each day, each hour, each minute in any learning situation, influences lives. Lives are forever altered in one direction or another.

She believes what she is doing should make a difference in the lives of persons she touches. She understands the opportunity and welcomes it with eagerness and passion. The environment creates an expectation of success and change. All are expected to be changed by the interactions between and among them.

The purpose is to help learners make positive changes in their lives. The environment helps students to see the beauty in their lives. It helps them to create and enhance that beauty. It expects the best, demands the best, and does not accept excuses for less. There is belief in the internal strength of the individual learner. Personal gifts are maximized.

The environment respects the integrity of each person; all who are together expect it for each other. There are only winners. They all model the idea that education is important and that it will enhance their lives. Whatever the subject, discipline, topic, or activity, the students are learning to broaden their view of themselves and their world. They cannot touch each other in such an environment and not be positively changed. That alone is acceptable.

The *secret* lies in the classroom and in the hearts and minds of those who are there together. Lives there are forever altered. Yes, a life is changed during every minute of every encounter in every classroom or elsewhere in any school or learning situation. We, all of us, need to make clear that we accept the responsibility of helping each person become all that she/he can become. We must allow them to go beyond the beaches to explore their own horizons. That is our high and holy task.

EPILOGUE

For many years I have been interested in the functioning of the brain. I always have believed intuitively and otherwise that to understand more about learning, I would have to know more about the brain. Because knowing more about learning was fundamental to any improvement in my teaching, learning more about the brain was both fascinating and necessary. As I look back over some of my earlier writings, presentations, and talks in this area, I can see that my quest for tying it all together has been a constant one. How can I know more about how my people learn? All the writing in this section is from those early writings thoughts, presentations, and conversations many years ago.

I am reminded of an admonition from T.H. Huxley: "Sit down before fact like a little child, and be prepared to give up every preconceived notion, follow humbly wherever and to whatever abyss Nature leads, or you shall learn nothing."

This means suspending our assumptions, putting them out in front of us for examination both by self and others. This is not an easy task; when we think that we have, we need to examine the amount of change that has taken place in our thinking. How much are we really hanging on to our old ideas? To examine this question requires a very different look at how we came to believe what we do. We have all looked on the surface—stereotypes, bias, prejudice, attitudes, values, affective opinions—names given to those areas that we examined. How did we come to hold these ideas and pictures about our personal universe, our "reality"?

Each experience that we have is stored in the brain. In the 1920s, researchers thought specific memories were stored in specific locations. Penfield's operations on the brains of epileptics caused him to believe that the response of the patients to electrical stimulation of various parts of the brain was due to recorded earlier experiences.

Subsequent research by Karl Lashley and others failed to confirm Wilder Penfield's engram theory; the research to the contrary proved that memories were distributed throughout the brain. They were not found at a specific site. But this nonlocalization of memories seemed unexplainable. How could this possibly be? Karl Pribrim continued his belief that memories were distributed. When he discovered the description of the first hologram construction in the mid 1960s, he felt that it might provide the solutions to the puzzle of the distribution of memories.

HOLOGRAMS

A hologram is three-dimensional and each piece of a holograph contains all the information that is present in the whole. Pribram reasoned that it was possible that every part of the brain could contain all of the information; therefore, each part of the brain could contain all the information necessary to recall any memory. This would allow memories to be distributed throughout the brain, not localized. The question then was how the brain could store so much in such a little space.

It has been calculated that a person during an average lifetime stores 280,000,000,000,000,000,000,000 (280 quintillion) bits of information in the brain. Holograms possess the capacity for such amazing storage capability. If the angle at which two lasers strike a piece of photographic film is changed, many different images may be recorded on the same surface. Using this method, it is estimated that a one-inch square of film could store the information in fifty Bibles. Think of the complexity and capacity of such an enormous storehouse.

It is interesting to speculate about the potential holographic storage capacity of the brain where each individual part is a part of the whole and the whole is in each part. Each experience we have is stored in the brain. This is consistent with much research that tells us that memories are stored throughout the brain rather than a specific site. This also helps us to understand the more recent research on plasticity of the brain.

DISSIPATIVE STRUCTURES

Another concept that has held great interest for me is the brain as a dissipative structure. Scientists have long believed that all things go in the direction of greater disorder. For instance, a new engine with its exact tolerances, has a maximum amount of disorder. However, as it begins to wear, disorder (randomness) increases. The heat of the engine causes the molecules to move more; as they collide with each other, they are knocked into random paths. Total randomness is chaos. As the engine transforms energy into work, it is unable to give as much energy as it consumes. Thus energy is lost and the friction ultimately wears out the parts—the engine becomes more disordered in the process.

Until chemist Ilya Prigogine concluded that order arises because of disorder, not despite it, and that life emerges out of entropy not against it, this had been a very difficult question. Prigogine discovered that not all things become disordered; some develop a more ordered arrangement. He called these spontaneously appearing ordered systems dissipative structures. Prigogine won a Nobel Prize for unraveling this mystery.

Prigogine realized that the law of thermodynamics that dictated that things would run down, tend toward randomness and chaos, has been applied to closed systems, systems that do not have a flow of energy between the environment and the system. Prigogine reasoned that living systems, human beings, are always open systems; they are systems far from a state of equilibrium. They adjust in numerous ways to their environment. He was fascinated with these systems that could fix themselves, learn new ways of doing things, could bring order out of chaos, and order out of disorder.

Dissipative structures maintain their structure from an energy flow from the outside. Prigogine used the metaphor of a windsock. As the breezes flow through the windsock, the structure becomes unpredictable, unstable—shaped and created by the energy that passes through the system. If the energy, the wind, stops, the windsock ceases to exist as a three-dimensional, open system.

The more complex the system, the more entropy (the amount of randomness in a system) it must dissipate. Dissipative structures are largely formed by the energy and matter flowing through them. Similarly, our bodies are not simply preexistent structures that pass energy and matter through them in the form of food, water, oxygen and so on; they literally are the energy and matter that flow through them. Dissipative structures are flow. They are created and flourish in high-energy, unstable, volatile, far-from-equilibrium environments. These unstable situations appear to be able to self-organize

195

into higher level structures.

We might say, so what?

Imagine the brain as an open system, a dissipative structure, of the highest order. Think of the brain as an enormously complex structure swept with oscillations of chemical and electrical waves. Think of the brain as a self-organizing, complicated and intricate network of cells that are so sensitive that they can be destabilized by a change in permeability of just a few of its billions and billions of cells.

How can we consider the brain as a dissipative structure? For a structure to be a dissipative structure it must be open, far from equilibrium, and autocatalytic. First, a dissipative structure can remain open only by remaining open to a flowing interchange of matter and energy with the environment. Second, there must be a high-energy environment with a constant influx of new energy. This is necessary for the process of self-organization that allows the system to fluctuate and dissipate the resulting entropy into the environment. Near equilibrium, the system would become like a closed system (increased entropy). Third, it is autocatalytic—from the words "auto" (self) and "catalyst" (an agent that helps change other things while not becoming changed itself). Elements of the system are self-reproducing, self-reinforcing; an example in living systems is the ability of cells to reproduce themselves.

The brain meets all these requirements. Certainly it is a most prodigious energy user. It comprises two percent of the body weight yet uses more than twenty percent of all the oxygen taken into the body. The brain functions far from equilibrium where various parts have clearly fixed functions. Neuroscientists no longer believe that the

196

brain operates like a telephone, a computer, or any machine. The energy that flows into the brain is transformed into ideas, thoughts, emotions, not predictable actions like an on-off machine.

It is this autocatalytic nature of the dissipative structure brain that tells us why the same simple stimulus given to two different persons can cause such tremendously different reactions. One person experiencing this destabilization will organize at a higher level; another who is not capable of such reorganization will experience chaos. All the possibilities are there in this magnificent structure, the brain.

For anyone who hears the story of Saul on the road to Damascus, there's a fascination about the happenings. Saul's brain is destabilized, torn loose from its mooring, and no longer able to deal with the input. Saul does not eat or drink for days; he is totally blind. But suddenly he is able to put the pieces together in a new way that is more complex, more interconnected, and more evolved—a higher level. The new way is able to handle the energy passing through.

These ideas are very pertinent to potential for creative thinking and also relative to people who resist any experience or idea that is new. For those persons who are artists and creative thinkers, there will be more fluidity, more susceptibility to disorder, and more turmoil possible. As a consequence there will be richer, denser neural networks, more synaptic possibilities, and a greater range of thoughts, feelings, and sensations. On the other hand, for those who never doubt their ideas, who are always right, who do not want anything new to happen in their lives, there will be stagnation; thermodynamically speaking, they turn their brains into a closed system. They are like an engine, a stone near equilibrium status, with a brain like a rock, never destabilized, never a new idea or feeling.

Through the years as I have continued my interest and study of the brain to learn more about learning and teaching, I feel as if I am being thrust into new waters, new swimming holes, trying to learn new strokes to get to shore, trying to understand the essence of a new concept or idea. Or perhaps I am on an expedition without a map.

I must admit that there was often joy and exhilaration in the cold of new waters; there was also excitement in the warmth of the knowledge of the new paradigms found in the strange waters off shore. Sometimes my intuition told me that the waters were strange because I had been swimming in the familiar waters of Newtonian principles and Cartesian philosophy. Granted, often these new waters were unfriendly; I was told to get real, to be objective, and use the scientific method, and I would find safe haven.

And yet I kept going back to the strange seas and lakes and trying to find other like-minded souls to go swimming with me. As I looked at my quest for answers to teaching and learning, something inside kept asking me to look. As I looked at nature and the universe about me, the questions were always there. Fortunately, during my professional career and personal life, I have had the good fortune to find new swimming holes, to be thrust into waters not always comfortable, to find swimming partners, to find the alligators and the crocodiles, to see the beauty of sun and moon and stars, the flowers and the animals that love strange waters, too.

Yes, I have returned to the old swimming holes. Most of all I have often had to keep half of me swimming in the old hole and half in the new one as I teach and learn about both. Students, colleagues, and friends have looked at me with that look that says, "But I don't know how to swim; I don't even know where that swimming hole is;

I'm not going to jump into strange and murky waters."

OLD SWIMMING HOLES

Descartes based his view of the universe on two distinct and separate divisions: mind and matter. His material universe was nothing but a machine with a set of mechanical laws that explained how everything was arranged and how all things worked. This view was ascribed to all living things. Human beings were machines, mechanistic beings, whose parts operated on the mechanical laws of his universe. This was the conceptual framework that Newton accepted—a swimming hole of machine parts.

Newton proceeded to create mathematical formulas for these mechanistic and reductionistic views. Newton's swimming hole was based on absolute time and absolute space. All physical events took place in absolute space, empty and independent of any phenomena occurring within it. Changes in the physical world were explained in terms of absolute time, a separate dimension. Newton's indestructible objects that moved in absolute time and absolute space were solid material particles—the building blocks of all matter. This is a very familiar scientific swimming hole.

From the seventeenth century to the end of the nineteenth, the Newtonian and Cartesian models dominated the thinking of all scientists. Researchers accepted the mechanistic, reductionistic, view of the universe; their theories and assumptions were based on these premises. What they believed, they saw. What they taught us, we believed.

We based our teaching and learning on the belief that understanding the parts would give us an understanding of the whole. I don't know about you, but sometimes I got bad cramps swimming in that water. My views of nature around me and my formal study of physiology, anatomy, and biology were often at odds with what I saw and felt. My time as an athlete and a teacher of physical education kept prodding me about whole beings—whole systems. As a biology teacher, my view of nature and living things did not fit the mechanical model; my view has always been more systems oriented.

We must be willing to try new swimming holes. Educational institutions have long tried to be as objective about programs and leadership as their science peers. We now must be honest about our universe and use the science available to us. In organizations we build structures that we want to be permanent. In nature we see that there is an implicit faith that there are many ways to exist and maintain integrity. Look to the clouds, the streams, the new and old paths of animals, sunsets and sunrises. Each is what it is, but with special diversity and beauty, with fluctuation and change. The Greeks had a word for this self-integrity—autopoiesis.

We have already talked of Prigogine's work on dissipative structures. He reasoned that living systems are always open systems; they are systems far from a state of equilibrium. They are adjusting to their environment, fixing themselves, finding new ways of doing things, bringing order out of disorder, order out of chaos. They are self-organizing systems.

CHAOS AND COMPLEXITY THEORY

The theory of chaos is about systems; it crosses lines necessarily. The global nature of chaos theory and the subsequent blurring of lines do not allow us to think in typical (accepted) scientific, linear, and logical ways. To physicists, economists, biologists, mathematicians, and computer scientists, chaos has become a science of process rather than a fixed state; it is a state of becoming rather than a state of being. Chaos crosses the lines that have separated the disciplines.

Chaos theory helps us understand that the world is neither orderly and in Newtonian fashion completely predictable, nor is it disorderly and completely random. Complexity theory helps us understand the working of dynamic, self-organizing complex systems. Complexity theory is still not easily defined; research is still trying to define this concept that defies all conventional categories.

Scientists have come to recognize a balance point that they call the "edge of chaos." This point is where systems neither lock in place nor dissolve into a state of chaotic turbulence. Scientists suggest that it is at this edge where new ideas and concepts are challenging the status quo and where old ideas and theories will be discarded or changed.

What we know today about chaos theory is largely the result of imaginative mathematics and the accessible power of computers. This new thinking and research present a universe that is deterministic, obeying the fundamental physical laws, but with a predisposition for disorder, complexity and unpredictability. Chaos is order without predictability. Computers have allowed us to see this. Systems may last for long periods of time, but eventually there seems to be a pull from "chaotic attractors" toward a new shape that the computers have been able to capture.

Chaos theory helps us swim in the water between Newtonian determinism and reductionism and the unpredictability and indeterminism of quantum physics.

SPACE AND FIELDS

Newton's world of space was emptiness, but we now believe that space is not empty. As suggested by many quantum scientists, space is the basic ingredient of the universe. There is more of it than anything else. In the quantum world, space is no longer a void. It is thought to be filled with invisible. non-visible structures called fields that are the basic structure of the universe.

Early scientists working in this space and field area concentrated on space rather than particles. They learned that in the quantum world, the idea of fields became enticing and offered theoretical, useful constructs. Scientists have described these fields as tasteless and odorless, as invisible, inaudible and intangible. Because we cannot experience them through our five senses, we need to use other understandable metaphors to understand field theory. Some suggest they resemble an ocean filled with invisible structures that connect with each other.

Fields are not empty; space is not empty. We fill the fields with messages. We help to create the structures of the fields with our thoughts. Every person in the classroom (the organization) helps to create the environment, the ocean of invisible, interconnected structures.

INFORMATION AND COMMUNICATION

In this new exploration of the universe, communication is a very different thing from what we have been taught. We have treated information as a thing, a quantity transmitted and received from one place to another by one means or another. The linear nature of the sender and receiver conceptual structure we have learned does not fit the new nonlinear understanding of our universe. Communication becomes a different swimming hole.

"Walk the talk" takes on some very important new and scientific meanings. We cannot say one thing and do another; our behavior comes from our thoughts. They are out there and being picked up in these fields of energy.

When we consider that quantum entities can be particles or waves, we must pause and ponder about this. If the property is present because we decide to measure it, it becomes an important quality for us to think about. For many scientists, the universe is participatory—we create the present through our observation. This means that when we measure we are not neutral.

And what does all this mean to our enchanted place? I'm not certain, but I know that all of these areas need to be explored more. I know that all of these areas are important to understand the functioning of the human brain, the energy fields created by our thoughts, and the interesting thought about how holograms fit into the learning

203

issues. One thing I feel is certain: Everything is connected. We are pathfinders trying to find the trails and oceans and mountains that will help us know more about our personal investment and commitment to building enchanting places for all of our sons and daughters longing for themselves.

USEFUL BOOKS TO READ OR REFERENCE

Begley, Sharon. *Train Your Mind, Change your Brain*. Ballantine, Books, New York. 2007

Byrne, Rhonda. *The Secret*. Atria Books, New York. 2006

Christensen, Clayton M, Michael B. Horn and Curtis W. Johnson. *Disrupting Class, How Disruptive Innovation Will Change the Way the World Learns*. McGraw Hill, San Francisco. 2008

Doidge, Norman. *The Brain That Changes Itself.* The Penguin Group. New York. 2007

Hicks, Esther and Jerry. *The Law of Attraction*. Hay House, Carlsbad, California. 2006

Hicks, Esther and Jerry, *Ask and It Is Given*. Hay House, Carlsbad, California. 2004

Hawking, David R. *The Hidden Determinants of Human Behavior*. Hay House, Carlsbad, California. 2002

Iacoboni, Marco. *Mirroring People*. Farrar, Straus and Giroux, New York. 2008

Lipton, Bruce H. *The Biology of Belief.* Elite Books, Santa Rosa, California, 2005

Taylor, Sandra Anne. *Quantum Success*. Hay House, Carlsbad, California. 2006

Senge, Peter and others. *Schools That Learn*. Doubleday, New York. 2000

Zull, James E. *The Art of Changing the Brain, Exploring Teaching by Exploring the Biology of the Brain*. Stylus, Sterling, Virginia. 2002

There are many other books about the brain, the mind, multiple intelligences, differentiated instruction, and teaching and learning that influenced my thinking and my behavior over the many years in education. There are books by Capra, Samples, Maxwell, Thoreau, Emerson and so many others. Thoreau said, "Only that day dawns to which we are awake." So it is with our reading. Jon Kabat-Zinn wrote a book called "Wherever You Go, There You Are." Often we forget that as we learn and teach. He suggests that we often forget, "that we are here, where we already are, and that we are in what we are already in." That's what we have to work with. We are where you are; that's the only place that we can start.

.

ABOUT THE AUTHOR...

Sylvia (Sy) Tucker has held
positions as teacher, counsel-
or, administrator, professor,
and dean for more than six
decades in public elementary
and secondary schools and
private and public universi-
ties. She is currently serving her fourth four-
year term on a local school board. Dr. Tucker
is the recipient of many awards and honors
and remains active in her personal and professional communities. She offers this book
in gratitude for the incredible opportunities
and experiences she has had in her life. It
is her sincere hope that an idea or two will
help those who read it create enchanting
and joyous places of learning.

LaVergne, TN USA
31 January 2011
214670LV00006B/187/P

9 780984 483709